REBOUND
SUCCEED
AND WIN

10 SIMPLE HABITS TO TRANSFORM YOUR LIFE

KARMA BUTLER

CONTENTS

ACKNOWLEDGMENTS

This is my heartfelt thank you for guiding, developing, and supporting the creation of *Rebound, Succeed, and Win.* Your time, talents, and partnership are deeply appreciated. I will remain forever grateful for your belief in me and in our shared vision—that together, we can make a positive impact on the lives of those striving for self-growth and greatness.

Karren Butler - #1 Mom

Eddie Butler - #1 Dad

Wesley Breaux - UX Design Consultant

Andrew Francis - Cover Hair Stylist

Britt Smith - Cover Photographer

Amber Henderson - Cover Makeup Artist

Rica Brex - Cover Graphic Designer

Camille Pen - Editor

Lilian.db - UI Designer

Muzammil F. - Formatter

FOREWORD

If you want your days to be filled with joy, meaning, and a sense of purpose — while still feeling refreshed and rewarded—then you're in the right place.

Feeling sad, lost, lonely, overwhelmed, or just unsure about where your life is headed? You're not alone. These emotions are part of the human experience, but you don't have to live in fear or uncertainty.

Having the right tools and strategies to shift direction, push through challenges, and stay intentional with every move you make and every breath you take can change everything. Your success, health, wealth, and love life all depend on it.

In this book, I lay out guided steps and actions to help you build 10 simple yet powerful habits that will set you up to win every single day. They say the fastest way to move forward, succeed, and cut down the time spent failing, falling, and making mistakes is to learn from those who have already been there—those who come back to share their knowledge and experiences in the areas that matter most to you.

That's exactly what I'm doing in the chapters ahead. I'm showing up boldly to awaken, inspire, challenge, and impact your life.

The best advice I can give you? Keep an open mind, open your heart, absorb like a sponge, and be honest—with yourself and with others. That's how you'll get the most out of this book.

You are free to explore this book however you like—there's no need to read the chapters in order. Each chapter holds something that will connect with you in its own way, and that connection doesn't have to follow a set sequence. Life itself isn't presented in a straight line from start to finish, so why should this book be?

Take hold of the insights, personal development tools, skill sets, and character-revealing strategies in these pages at your own pace, in your own way. Enjoy getting to know yourself better without the pressure of reading traditionally—approach this book with a fresh mindset. Get what you need, when you need it, and how you need it.

Be bold, be brave, and be brilliant as you work through the strengthening exercises at the end of each chapter—they are the foundation of your growth. And even though we may never meet in person, I am incredibly proud of you for recognizing your own desire to learn and evolve. I encourage you to share the knowledge and skills you gain from this book with those you admire, adore, and love.

Many of the stories in the pages ahead are lighthearted, funny, and filled with laughter. Others are difficult and deeply personal—stories that were uncomfortable to share, moments that were sad, scary, and even tear-filled. But I believe with all my heart that by sharing my journey with you, both the mistakes and the victories, you'll find lessons that resonate.

My greatest hope is that through this book, you'll grow more confidently and easily into the best version of yourself, step into your next level, and embrace all that you are meant to be.

The world is yours to shape. Create the masterpiece of your life with your heart and soul. I want you to rebound. I want you to succeed. I want you to win!

—Karma

Chapter 1:

GET THE RESULTS YOU WANT AND STAND OUT FROM THE CROWD

A brand-new, crisp, light-blue textured button-down long-sleeve shirt, complemented with a contrasting light and dark blue diamond-patterned power necktie, had a sharp look on my chest. A dark grey dress suit, polished shiny shoes, and a black leather briefcase were the final touches that were meant to present me well for this lifetime opportunity of becoming a manager with Houston's Restaurants.

I was on board Southwest Airlines, flying from my home in Los Angeles, California, to an interview in Scottsdale, Arizona. I had just completed almost one year of manager-in-training courses and an internship program with one of America's most prestigious restaurant chains. They paid for my round-trip flights to and from one of their main restaurants near their corporate office in Scottsdale, Arizona. I felt like I had been handed the golden ticket to a lifetime opportunity, as I had never before been flown on an airplane round trip in a single day, fully paid for by a company.

When I landed in Scottsdale, I was met by a representative from their corporate office who drove me to their restaurant. I was given a tour of the restaurant and worked side-by-side in a station of the kitchen with one of their chefs. This was part of my evaluation for the interview. I was then able to sit down with one of the company's Executives of Operations for my official one-on-one interview, which, in my personal opinion, went downhill fast. What seemed like a golden lifetime ticket opportunity at this moment seemed to turn into a derogatory interrogation.

The Executive of Operations proceeded to tell me that their company only seeks graduates from college with a degree in culinary arts or hospitality. He continued to belittle me, reminding me that I had only one year of college as a dance major at the California Institute of the Arts and a resume from stage, television, and film. He told me that I seemed to be nothing more than a talented entertainer and that he didn't understand why I wanted to build a career with their company as a restaurateur.

I was in shock at this point, as his quick and pointed summary of my life took me by surprise. I became agitated and shifted into a higher gear with my verbal response, but I remained extremely professional. I had been coached and mentored on how to conduct myself during this interview, so I proceeded carefully, even though I was internally enraged.

I politely reminded the executive that I had been selected by the company to join their manager internship program because of my dedication and performance as their top-ranked server at their premier restaurant in Santa Monica, California. I continued to respectfully inform the Executive of Operations that I had succeeded in and passed their three-month manager internship program, which was honestly like a Navy SEAL boot camp.

I kept the conversation moving forward, acknowledging that my background and education were primarily in entertainment and performing arts. I passionately explained that it was a personal choice of mine to partner with Houston's Restaurants and pursue restaurant operations at the highest level in the industry with the company. I agreed to undergo the rigorous and demanding schedule that, at this time, consumed most of my time almost every day of every week.

I shared with the Executive of Operations that I did have other options to continue pursuing my path in the arts. I made it clear through communication that I was committed to becoming a leader with the company by choice, out of passion and dedication. The Executive of Operations didn't seem to display any reactions or emotions, and then informed me that the interview had ended.

After the interview, I was given a meal of choice from the restaurant's menu, which was top-tier, upscale, and refined All-American Cuisine. In the early evening, I was driven back to the airport by a member of their office team, and I flew back to Los Angeles. During the flight home, I became at ease in my mind, realizing that it was most likely I had not secured the position I had interviewed for, based on how I personally perceived the interview had gone so poorly.

When I returned to the restaurant in Los Angeles where I had completed my internship, I had to meet with the General Manager. To my surprise, the General Manager congratulated me on passing my interview in Scottsdale with the Executive of Operations. I was offered a $45,000 per year salary and a position in their official Manager In Training courses, which were about eight months long and included a bonus moving allowance to use for my relocation to Scottsdale, Arizona. All of this fortunately happened for me during the exciting years of my young twenties.

I felt tears of shock and happiness welling up in my eyelids, but I held them back when I heard the incredible news. I then shook the General Manager's hand—the one who had spent many months personally investing in me and grooming me for promotion—and proudly accepted the offer. Less than a week after accepting the offer, I packed everything I owned into a U-Haul rental truck, hitched my vehicle to a tow bed attached to the truck, and boldly, alone, moved from Los Angeles, California, to Scottsdale, Arizona.

In Scottsdale, I had my own two-bedroom apartment in an upscale community, with all moving costs and deposits paid by the company. At this time, I was 23 years old, the only Black person in their Manager In Training program, and was among a class of about thirty other rising professionals, all with college degrees in culinary arts or hospitality—except me. I was on the management team and living in a plush, prominent city in Arizona, all thanks to Houston's Restaurants, but I knew I was still somehow different from the others having the same experience.

I was on my way to achieving my personal goal of becoming the General Manager of a restaurant chain. At this time, I was doing this with the most well-known leader and most highly respected restaurant industry training program for restaurant operators. I had a potential six-figure yearly income quickly approaching ahead of me.

I completed the army-like, chef-centered manager-in-training program, and after graduating from the program, I accepted a $50,000 per year salary offer as a full-time assistant manager at the same restaurant where I had trained in Scottsdale. I was simply stunned that I had earned a $5,000 pay increase in just a few months of taking on the new role, and as a 23-year-old, I felt like I had won the lottery.

I sweated all day, every day. In the hot Arizona summer, with extreme, dry, one-hundred-degree average heat in the desert area of Scottsdale, I was sweating in the kitchen in my chef coat. I was also sweating while walking constant circles through the dining room, ensuring prompt and polished service for the guests. The most dreadful sweating came while I was quality-checking every single entrée delivered through the kitchen expeditor area, as the manager ensuring consistency, quality, and proper plate presentation for every customer's starter, appetizer, entrée, and dessert—while wearing the required suit and power tie.

Life was more than incredible career-wise and financially. Life became very lonely personally, as I had no friends or family in Arizona, except for a few co-managers. At night, after getting off work—usually a little before midnight—I would try to enjoy the beautiful balcony view I had of the city at my apartment, complemented with a relaxing glass of wine. The temperature was still near one hundred degrees, even at midnight. Sweat would constantly drip down my forehead and cascade down my face into the posh glass of wine I was drinking, which would then become tainted from my own sweat just from sitting still on the balcony.

I had also become accustomed to always being surrounded by sand, dryness, and desert life, where there wasn't a beach or even a natural lake that I was familiar with, as I had lived in California.

I shared the many concerns and struggles of the new lifestyle I was living in Scottsdale with my boss and requested to be moved back to California while still working for the company. Luckily, the company had just opened their newest concept, a Euro-Style Bistro, in Newport Beach, California, next to the beautiful and exclusive town of Laguna Beach. I was offered a $65,000 per year salary for the opportunity. I accepted the offer before they even completed all the details because I desperately wanted to leave Arizona and move back to California, where there were breezes, beaches, and naturally grown palm trees.

At the time, what I didn't realize was that I had been given another $15,000 pay raise within a few months of receiving the previous one, and was now headed to the company's newest concept that had all eyes on it.

Once again, in first-class style, the company paid for all of my moving costs and home-living deposits. In just a few short days after accepting the offer, I moved from Scottsdale, Arizona, to Newport Beach, California.

I arrived at the new restaurant, which had just completed construction and opened its doors to the public, alongside the mall anchors of Bloomingdale's, Macy's, Neiman Marcus, and Nordstrom, in the renowned Fashion Island Shopping Mall in luxurious Newport Beach. I met with my new general manager, and to my surprise, he was the only other Black manager, besides myself, that I had encountered during my time with this restaurant company. He was clearly at the top level of his leadership, and I was eager to learn from him.

He graciously welcomed me onto his team with open arms and told me that if I performed well in my role as an assistant manager at this location, I would be on track for promotions that would assist me in my goal of becoming a general manager with the company. He continued to share insider information, telling me that the current store's location was the newest concept within the company. He also shared that all of the high-level executives of the company frequented the restaurant we were managing, giving me the prime opportunity to showcase my culinary and service leadership skills, which would help me get promoted to general manager.

Over the next few months, I worked 60-70 hours per week and was being groomed to be an assistant general manager with an entry salary of $75,000 per year. The beach life in Newport Beach was incredibly fulfilling, and I often ventured next door to Laguna Beach, which had some of the most breathtaking beach views I had ever seen. It was so beautifully mesmerizing living there that the $1,200 per month rent for my tiny studio apartment didn't bother me one bit.

I often traveled back to Los Angeles to visit my best friend from college, Jennifer, and other friends and family, as Los Angeles was only a few hours' drive from Newport Beach. Life was incredible, living in this first-class city, working for a first-class company in my young twenties, and I was quickly on my way to becoming a six-figure yearly-earning general manager.

Any new restaurant opening requires much longer work hours and routines than a restaurant that has been open and operating for a long time and is well established. I was the bar manager at this restaurant in Newport Beach, and when a bartender would call out for their shift, my general manager would call me in to cover it. This was often on my days off or replacing an opening morning bartender's shift, which was scheduled before my 10-hour closing manager shift, so I worked about 15 hours. This cycle continued for several months. The constantly changing demands from my regional manager and the company's executives for their new precious baby, their new Euro-styled Bistro, became mentally and physically exhausting and no longer enjoyable—even with the great salary I had.

During a one-on-one meeting with my regional manager, he became so enraged with our conversation that he started yelling at me and swearing at me. I personally hadn't remembered my own parents yelling and cursing at me the way he was, and I was deeply offended by his unprofessional behavior. That was the straw that broke the camel's back, and I had enough. No two-week notice was given, and without hesitation—feeling drained, wrecked, and unappreciated—I quit. My six-figure potential general manager opportunity with the company was gone in the blink of an eye after one conversation.

I later moved back to the East Coast to my hometown of Chesapeake, Virginia, where I stayed with my mom and dad in our home, and they supported me in regrouping and starting the next chapter of my life. Chesapeake, Virginia, and Los Angeles, California, are like night and day in many ways. I was now living back in my suburban hometown, where my parents had built their dream retirement home. It was also the place where I had attended two high schools simultaneously—one for academics and one for performing arts.

Chesapeake, Virginia, is definitely not bursting at the seams with entertainment industry opportunities, but like most U.S. cities, it does have its fair share of national restaurant chains. Needing a job, my dad recommended that I apply at this brand-new restaurant being built in our city. The restaurant was enormous in size when I saw it while passing by several times on Greenbrier Parkway, still freshly back in town. It remained strange to me that I had never heard of the restaurant chain before in the West Coast restaurant industry, where I had been so involved.

I researched the restaurant chain and consulted other restaurateurs I knew, and they told me that it was a highly respected, popular, and growing chain, and that I would most likely enjoy working with them. It was a steakhouse chain called Texas Roadhouse.

Needing a job at the time was a high priority, so I followed the advice of my parents and restaurant industry friends and walked into the hiring trailer just outside the new restaurant being built. I personally submitted an application. I was still very burnt out and maxed out from my recent manager journey that I had just quit on the West Coast, so I applied as a server, not wanting too many responsibilities.

The hiring manager, named Guy, was extremely nice and had high energy. He was tossing a football around outside with applicants, including me, while we waited to be interviewed. During my time interviewing with the hiring manager, who I thought was very down-to-earth and easy to converse with, we had light conversations and seemed to connect very well.

After reviewing my resume and speaking with me, he immediately took me into the back room of the hiring trailer and introduced me to the managing partner of the newly built restaurant. The managing partner, Jim, was highly impressed with my restaurant industry resume and spoke highly of his knowledge of Houston's Restaurants, the previous restaurant chain I had managed.

I remember telling Jim, the managing partner, that I didn't want to be a restaurant manager anymore, but I still had a passion for the industry. He seemed to intentionally disregard my honesty and told me that he could teach me "how to run one of these" and that I was capable of doing so. I reminded him that I was applying for a server position. He then proceeded to tell me to take his personal cell phone number and enter it into my phone. I found this very strange, as most operators don't give their personal cell phone numbers to applicants during hiring interviews.

He then told me he was going to take me on a tour of the inside of the restaurant. He shared with me that they needed someone in charge of marketing for the restaurant and that he thought I would be a great fit for the position. I also found this strange because the restaurant still seemed to be under construction, and I didn't see the other applicants being taken inside the building.

I followed the Managing Partner, Jim, into the building. I was struck with awe and filled with bliss by the smell of the new cedar wood that permeated the interior, the vastness of the layout, the impressiveness of the culture they shared with me, and the overall design of the concept. While on the tour, he stopped to introduce me to the Market Partner, Jesse, who was in the building among the construction workers.

After coming from a restaurant chain where I had to work all day in a chef coat or a suit and tie, to a restaurant chain where I could wear jeans and a t-shirt, line dance every hour, and be a server with no responsibilities other than serving and doing marketing work for the restaurant, I jumped on board with the opportunity quickly at that moment.

Inside the restaurant that same day I applied, Jim and Guy offered me the server position I wanted, along with the local store marketer position they were seeking. The local store marketer position, which I was unfamiliar with, would provide me the chance to become the face of the restaurant, doing marketing inside and outside the location within the community. I accepted the offer, and it literally changed my life forever.

After the grand opening, the restaurant was a huge success in Chesapeake, Virginia, and it quickly outperformed competing restaurants nearby week after week. As time progressed, I became their top-ranked server, but mostly worked in the role of local store marketer, booking catering, special events, and working with local businesses, radio stations, and television news stations.

It wasn't too long before Texas Roadhouse offered me the opportunity to be a full-time salaried manager on their team. With my previous manager journey that seemed to end in misery, bruises, and heartbreak, my mind was telling me to say "no thank you," absolutely not, and never again. However, my heart and spirit were pumping with joy and excitement, as I had developed a sincere and profound love for working with this amazing restaurant company during the first year of the Chesapeake, Virginia, restaurant opening. To this day, I remain in awe of how Texas Roadhouse positively impacted the lives of our hired opening team, myself included, and the community of Chesapeake through legendary food and service.

Partnering with the Chesapeake Police Department, under the leadership of the iconic Lt. J.R. (Randy) LeFebvre— a legend in my eyes— our team was able to provide support to the Special Olympics in our local community. It was extremely fulfilling to be on the ground with a strong social circle of passionate, driven organizational leaders, all striving to elevate and inspire the community. Hand-cut steaks and Special Olympic athletes somehow made a perfectly magical blend.

Surprisingly to myself, within a few short months of working at the restaurant, I accepted their offer to be a service manager, with an industry-competitive yearly salary. The time in my new position as service manager was extremely enjoyable and challenging in new, rewarding ways.

Jim, the managing partner of the restaurant, continued to inspire my growth with the company and even made an encouraging proclamation to me that he knew I could become Service Manager of the Year. As much as I was grateful for his encouragement and support of my restaurant career, I was still extremely scared and hesitant to pursue the dream-like goal of becoming a Managing Partner of America's top-rated steakhouse chain.

Texas Roadhouse has an extraordinary vision and a company-centered focus on the role of managing partner. A managing partner has partial ownership and can make operational decisions within the company's culture that best support employees, guests, and foster a strong connection to the community.

I quickly came to learn both the front of house (the dining room) and the back of house (the kitchen), and it was truly an exciting time in my life. Guests of the restaurant were in love with the overall concept. When I would meet random strangers and they found out that I was a manager at Texas Roadhouse, they often raved about the food and service. Most often, I would hear about their love for the fresh-baked bread and honey-cinnamon butter served with it. The guests' profound admiration for the company, repeated time and time again, internally confirmed that I had made the right choice in accepting the role of manager with the company.

Sadly, Jim was no longer the managing partner of the store I was at, and the second managing partner who had joined our team also didn't stay in the leading role for long. My current market partner approached me and had a meeting with me during this time. He shared the news that the second managing partner wasn't in the role anymore, and there was a new managing partner for our restaurant who was still in training. It would be several months before the newly appointed managing partner would complete his training and officially assume the role at our restaurant. My market partner, also named Jim, asked me to be the acting managing partner for the store for a few months until the assigned managing partner completed his training.

Wow! A dream of mine that I had given up on previously and was running away from had slapped me in the face. It was real, it was live, and it was the perfect opportunity to continue to grow with the company. During the next few months, I ran the Chesapeake restaurant as the acting managing partner to the best of my ability and became nicknamed by my team as "MP3," a short slang version for being the third person to become managing partner of the somewhat new restaurant.

Somehow, I had strangely fallen in line with my goal of becoming a general manager of a successful restaurant. Even better, I was being seen and recognized as a managing partner of America's #1 rated steakhouse chain. I rapidly grew as a leader, and our management team and employees worked incredibly hard to keep the restaurant growing and thriving. Eventually, the new managing partner, Peter, arrived, and I assisted in getting him settled into the restaurant. We had a great partnership, with him as the managing partner and me as the service manager.

From this brief experience that lasted several months, my drive to become a restaurant operator and owner—known as a managing partner—was alive and kicking. After enjoying my brief time as an acting managing partner, I shared with my market partner that I wanted to be considered as a candidate to become a managing partner with the company.

In 2009, four years into my employment with Texas Roadhouse, I was named a finalist for "Service Manager of the Year." It is one of the company's highest honors, as the top four service managers in the company. I was flown to New York City, ironically my place of birth and young childhood, for the yearly Managing Partner's Conference to receive my award. The week-long trip was red-carpet treatment from start to finish. During this trip, Texas Roadhouse truly made me feel like a king, and I will never forget how they made me feel appreciated, going well above and beyond to provide a lavish, life-long memorable, and impactful experience of gratitude.

Texas Roadhouse provided me a room all to myself at the renowned Waldorf Astoria in New York City for the week. I received a bonus check as an award, handed to me by the CEO/Founder of Texas Roadhouse, Kent Taylor. I also received congratulatory handshakes from other executives of the company while on stage receiving my award. The famous dancing Radio City Rockettes handed me my crystal award on stage at the iconic Radio City Music Hall, the same place the NFL had announced and celebrated their draft picks for many years. This experience was epic, iconic, and truly life-changing.

During the week-long conference, I had the opportunity to see other award-winning recipients, including the company's top meat cutters, be interviewed and featured on national television on the Today Show. I was also impressed to see the company's CEO, Kent Taylor, open the daily stock market on the New York Stock Exchange by ringing the bell, which was shown on larger-than-life-sized screens in the popular New York City Times Square.

I was wined and dined with gifts, private concerts, banquets, and private events while at the conference. There were privately chartered Staten Island Ferry boats that took us to an exclusive catered event at Ellis Island. On the island, there were many food stations offering foods from around the world. The food stations recognized the multicultural deep roots of the restaurant industry, as immigrants had years before migrated to New York City on boats from various parts of the world outside of the United States. This evening concluded at the end of the week-long conference with performances from celebrities at a waterfront stage and a firework show from the waters of the Hudson River that illuminated the skyline of New York City. It was breathtaking, uniquely marvelous, and I will never forget it.

To top it off, the home office of Texas Roadhouse placed a featured article in my local Hampton Roads, Virginia newspaper, *The Virginian-Pilot,* about me receiving the Service Manager of the Year Finalist award. Many phone calls from friends and family were received by my parents and me after the article was published. I was on cloud nine, or maybe even cloud twenty, and I felt like I was truly living a dream.

I tremendously enjoyed incredible experiences with Texas Roadhouse, which at this time had only been 4 years fresh for me. They mentored passion, partnership, integrity, and fun with purpose through leadership and entrepreneurship. This strongly propelled me to pursue becoming a managing partner with the company, and I unexpectedly found myself back on the path of pursuing my goal to become a restaurant owner/operator.

In the years following my life-changing, award-winning experience as Service Manager of the Year Finalist, I was invited as one of two candidates to interview for the position of managing partner for one of the restaurant chain's locations in the Washington, D.C. area. At this time, my tenure with the company was about 5 to 6 years. The other candidate for the position had come from an outside restaurant chain and had been with the company for about 1 year. Based on how long this employee had been with the company, I found myself questioning my position in the selection process, thinking that I should have been the person of choice for the position.

After the interview process, which involved two days of travel outside my home city of Chesapeake, VA, to Washington, D.C., as well as an overnight hotel stay, I returned home to my local restaurant. I was told by my market manager that I was not selected for the position and was encouraged not to be disappointed. I was more than disappointed—I was furious and saddened. The fact that a brand-new employee with the company had secured the managing partner position over me, someone who had been with the company for about six years, was devastating. I perceived that because my market partner and the newly hired managing partner had previously worked together at an outside restaurant chain, that was the reason the new incoming manager was selected instead of me.

As I reflect now on that experience, I respect that I was not the chosen candidate for the managing partner promotion. I should not have assumed that working for the company for several years would be the ultimate deciding factor in choosing me over the other candidate. I am very appreciative that I was considered for the position, and now I know, many years later, that it was extremely closed-minded and opinionated of me to be so angry about not getting the promotion. Truth be told, many years later, my market partner, Jim, continued to advocate for my growth within my restaurant career.

When I didn't get the promotion, I faced significant internal obstacles regarding my goal in the restaurant industry. At that time, I had enough. I was finished with giving so much of myself and striving so hard with everything that I had within me to climb the ranks in the company, only to be disappointed and shut out from not being promoted. It felt absolutely horrible.

During my personal time outside of being a service manager for the restaurant, I was actively fulfilling a dream of mine to produce an original talent variety television show. I connected with local business owners, performers, talent agents, directors, and an advertising agency to support me in producing and broadcasting the show.

While producing my first television show, I gained valuable knowledge through trial and error as an independent executive producer. I was extremely fascinated with the world of television production, and after broadcasting one episode of my self-created television show, I was hooked.

The restaurant industry was, of course, my main career, but I made time to produce my television show before and after my restaurant workdays, and on my days off from the restaurant. I found prolific joy and deep passion in producing television. After broadcasting the pilot episode of *Fever*, I realized that I had gained the basic knowledge and experience to produce a full television series.

While still on my entrepreneurial journey in restaurant operations and television production, I was moved to a different restaurant in Newport News, Virginia. I was now a kitchen manager, instead of a service manager. The plan, laid out by my market partner, was for me to become more well-versed in running all areas of the restaurant—both front of house and back of house—to assist me in getting promoted to managing partner. While I was the kitchen manager at this location, I was deep in the trenches of executive producing my second television concept, a four-episode broadcast series.

Karma Butler's American Dance Legend broadcast four thirty-minute episodes spread over four weeks on the CBS affiliate, WTKR. This network broadcasted to seven local cities in the southeastern part of Virginia, known as Hampton Roads. The television series received Nielsen ratings that averaged about 4,000 household viewers per episode. While this rating isn't high for a well-established television show, I was told that it had merit and was an impressive rating for a brand-new independent television broadcast series.

Managing a restaurant full-time while producing a television series at the same time was very stressful. After broadcasting my television series, which had become known as "ADL," local fans, viewers, and cast members continued to ask me when ADL Season 2 was coming out.

At first, I continually laughed at the idea of doing a second season due to the high stress level of being an executive television producer without any formal training. I had forced myself to learn everything about producing a television series from start to finish the hard way—by trial and error—and it was mentally and physically exhausting.

"

"Nothing in life that ranks as a high goal and offers great rewards comes easy."

After considering producing a second season of *American Dance Legend*, I realized it could be a once-in-a-lifetime opportunity to have my own television series that people actually liked and were passionate about supporting—both the cast members and the viewing of more episodes.

Nothing in life that ranks as a high goal and offers great rewards comes easy. I simply had to become more resilient at managing the stress and responsibility that came with being an independent executive television producer. After becoming comfortable with this internal turmoil, I made the decision to move forward and began producing *American Dance Legend* Season 2.

In 2012, *American Dance Legend* Season 2 grew to six episodes that were broadcast on a major television network affiliate, My Network TV. The second season, during production, faced many unforeseen challenges and obstacles. The ratings of the show didn't grow as anticipated. The Nielsen ratings of *American Dance Legend* Season 2 were about the same as the first season of the television series. As the executive producer of *American Dance Legend* Season 2, I can honestly share with you that it was not as successful as the first broadcast season.

It seemed to me that I had hit a concrete wall in my life. I was still a kitchen manager at a location that was extremely difficult for me to operate and succeed at. I hadn't achieved my goal of becoming a managing partner with Texas Roadhouse, and I was now seven years into my career with the company. I had a television series with potential to grow, but I felt like a failure. I was extremely sad every day for many months because of my own self-created obstacles.

In pursuit of my goal to grow and distribute my television series, *American Dance Legend*, I began reaching out to producers at large television production companies, also known as production houses. I didn't receive any responses and became somewhat depressed and lost in life during this time. Time passed, and it felt like a never-ending tunnel, but one day, a television producer in Orlando, Florida, responded to me by email.

The television producer who reached out to me had worked on several national television broadcasts, including the annual Disney Christmas Day Parade on ABC. He told me that he would be interested in meeting with me about a possible partnership for *American Dance Legend*. After hearing this exciting news, I quickly put in for a week of vacation time so that I could travel to Orlando to meet with the producer.

After meeting with him, it was decided that I would need to be in Orlando for an extended period of time to work side-by-side with the producer to grow the distribution of the show to more widespread broadcast television markets and to elevate the talent pool of dancers and choreographers for *American Dance Legend* Season 3.

I was faced with a decision: stay the course as a restaurant manager or step down from my salary at the restaurant and pursue, 100% all in, my dance reality television series. I was working as a kitchen manager at the time, on what seemed to be an endless pursuit to become a managing partner. The other attractive option was to move to Orlando and work with a high-profile television producer who could help me grow and broadcast my television series to larger, well-known major television networks and DMAs (Designated Market Areas) that broadcast across all fifty states.

It was one of the most difficult decisions I had to make in my life. After careful consideration, with input from friends and family, I concluded that I could always return to the restaurant company, but I might never again have the opportunity to produce my television series with a successful and high-profile television producer.

In the summer of 2012, I moved to Orlando, Florida, leaving my eight-year restaurant career with Texas Roadhouse to pursue a dream opportunity as the executive producer of *American Dance Legend*, with hopes of regional and national television broadcast distribution. This decision made me extremely nervous and uncomfortable, but to the core of my being, I was ready and willing to take the risk. I packed up my life into a U-Haul truck and quickly found myself living in a resort-style community in Kissimmee, Florida, known worldwide as the home of Disney World.

Now I was in Orlando, able to meet with the high-profile television producer who was going to partner with my show as often as he wanted to, with ease and convenience, to build our joint broadcast plan for *American Dance Legend* Season 3. Life seemed like it couldn't get any better at the time. I was living the dream of a lifetime, pursuing and achieving my ambitions, goals, and dreams.

I continued to call and email the producer over and over again with no response. At first, the lack of response lasted a few days, then a few weeks, and then it dragged on for several months. Sadly, after multiple attempts to reach out to the producer—by all means possible—I came to the realization that this opportunity and partnership was not going to happen. The producer who had offered me his time, partnership, talents, network, and passion completely outcast me, ignored me, and shut me out. This experience deeply hurt me, from my inner core to my outer flesh.

Here I was in uncharted territory, a brand-new city that felt like a foreign land to me, with no way back home to Virginia, where my mom, friends, colleagues, and family were. The reality hit me hard that I had no chance of producing Season 3 of my television series and that I had used up all the stocks, savings, and available funds I had accumulated over many years on one dead-end pipe dream.

Although Season 3 of *American Dance Legend* didn't happen as expected, I was energized by the incredible opportunity to work at the new Texas Roadhouse restaurant in Kissimmee, which was crushing the sales of all the other restaurant competitors in the area. It was truly amazing to be a part of the team and that restaurant, and I will never forget how our team all started together, stuck together, and built it together one guest at a time.

The passion of Texas Roadhouse in Kissimmee, Florida, is immediately felt when you walk in, and it speaks for itself through the legendary food and exceptional service, both unmatched in the area. I had the privilege of being a part of the foundation of the restaurant, which was often recognized throughout the year as the busiest location within the Texas Roadhouse family. This remains a tremendous honor.

To share a glimpse of the personal impact Texas Roadhouse has had on my life, they generously helped cover the cost of my father's funeral during an incredibly difficult time. Additionally, two locations in the Virginia market—Chesapeake and Yorktown—and the Florida market in Kissimmee, under the leadership of the one-and-only Adam Conrad, sponsored all three seasons of my television series, *American Dance Legend*.

It is rare for a company to support the personal dreams and goals of its employees, especially those that lie outside of the company's daily operations. Texas Roadhouse stands as a leader in the restaurant industry, passionately supporting and uplifting the lives of their employees, known as "Roadies." This truth is something I know firsthand, and I am just one of thousands of "Roadies" who proudly boast of my gratitude and the unforgettable experiences I've had with Texas Roadhouse.

During my time with the company, I had the opportunity to attend a training class in Louisville, Kentucky, with CEO/Founder Kent Taylor. Before the class began, Kent was on a ladder changing a light bulb in one of his 300+ restaurants. From the very start of this class, it was clear that no matter your position within the company, we were all expected to be fully involved and share in the daily operations of the business—a lesson exemplified by a CEO changing a light bulb on a ladder.

During the class, Kent shared with us that when his restaurant was struggling in its early years, long before it became the giant it is today, he didn't know what move to make next. He told us that failure was never an option. He took his famous ribs from his restaurant and began visiting all the businesses in his area, sharing both the legendary fall-off-the-bone ribs and the story of his restaurant.

Kent personally taught us to always remain persistent in our roles as operators, and to this day, I carry this invaluable habit into both my personal and work life. During challenging times in operations, we, as operators, would often ask ourselves, "WWKD?" This stood for: "What Would Kent Do?" The answer was always focused on persistence, overcoming the obstacle at hand.

A few years ago, I heard the heartbreaking news of Kent Taylor's passing. I collapsed on my bed and cried deeply for several hours. Though I had only met Kent a handful of times throughout my 13-year career with Texas Roadhouse, his personal impact on me—and how one individual can inspire the lives of so many through persistence in achieving their goals and dreams—was nothing short of extraordinary. Kent's success in building one of America's largest restaurant companies exemplified this perfectly. Thank you, Kent, for your persistence and for creating a path for so many— including myself—to follow toward entrepreneurship and success. I will always remain honored and grateful for the legendary Kent Taylor.

I want to share my personal and in-depth example of how years of persistence led me to achieve my goal of becoming a managing partner with America's #1 rated steakhouse chain. This journey of persistence is shared with you to help you remove your blinders and fully understand the profound impact that being persistent in achieving your personal goals, hopes, and dreams can have on your life. This one simple habit can truly transform your life.

Persistence is what will set you apart from the crowd, the noise of the world, and make you the obvious choice. It reveals your courage, your boldness, your grit, and your willingness to do what others won't. But being truly persistent, at times, will tear you down. It will break you into tiny pieces. It will make you want to quit and bring out the most uncomfortable emotions within you. However, on the other side of your persistence is the best version of yourself that you've never seen before, and I strongly encourage you to reach for that person waiting for you on the other side to realize your full potential. That person waiting for you is you! Be persistent.

Habit 1:

Be Persistent

Steps Toward Being Persistent

Identify the tasks you need to complete every day that will bring you closer to your goal. Once you identify these tasks, commit to completing them daily until it becomes a natural habit.

Understand why achieving your goals is important to you and only you. Ask yourself, "Why is this important to me?"

_____

_____

_____

_____

Be prepared for long days. To be at the top of your field, you must outwork everyone else in your circle and industry.

_____

_____

_____

_____

Quickly recognize your weaknesses and develop the resilience to overcome them.

_____

_____

_____

_____

_____

_____

Stay dedicated to your plan and follow through, even if it means temporarily shutting out the outside world.

_____

_____

_____

_____

Continuously find the willpower to push through and overcome any obstacles or roadblocks in your path.

Chapter 2:

OVERCOME YOUR FEARS AND BEAT YOUR COWARDLY LION

I n elementary school, in the suburbs of Philadelphia, I was a popular kid, or at least I think I was, thanks to my fun personality. I was charismatic, full of energy, and usually smiling.

Most of the day, I went to classes with the other students, like gym and music. However, for a small portion of the school day, for core subjects like reading and math, I was placed in a different classroom. I wasn't progressing at the same pace as the other students in my grade and needed extra time and attention to catch up on vital academic skills, including reading and writing.

The specialized class my teachers and parents agreed I should attend was called Chapter 1. It was much smaller than the other classes, with just a handful of students. Even in first grade, I understood that my learning capabilities were a little slower, and I was behind most of my classmates.

It was often hard to separate from my friends when it was time for Chapter 1 class. I felt like I was missing out on the fun of being with the larger group of students. I remember having to focus extremely hard to comprehend the materials my teachers were presenting in Chapter 1. Writing letters, spelling words, and understanding math were all extremely challenging for me, but I listened carefully to my teachers and did my best to overcome each learning hurdle.

I was never diagnosed as being disabled in any capacity, but oftentimes I felt somewhat disabled because people treated me differently due to being in the Chapter 1 class. You might think that the other kids would make fun of me or treat me differently since I was in a "special" learning class, but ironically, my homeroom teacher often treated me very differently from the other kids in her class.

She would often be curt and aggressive toward me, and I didn't see her treat the other kids in our homeroom the same way. But I just accepted the constant hostile communication and treatment she directed at me. She treated me as if I were the class clown.

One day, our homeroom was in the library, and as usual, this same teacher was being aggressive toward me. I don't remember damaging anything or being mean to anyone, but for whatever reason, she was upset with me as we walked down the hallway from the library back to our homeroom. She began yelling at me and called me a big jerk in front of all my classmates.

Internally, I tried to understand why this teacher was being so cruel to me. Was it because I was one of the only Black students at the school? Was it because I was having too much fun with the other students? Was it because I was in the Chapter 1 class? I kept asking myself these questions over and over again.

I was usually bubbly, bright, and full of smiles every day, but on one particular day, my parents noticed that I was very sad. When my mother and father asked why I wasn't in my usual happy mood, I shared with them the unpleasant experiences I had with my homeroom teacher. Both of my parents were deeply upset about what had happened. My mom was beyond angry when she found out that the teacher had outwardly and verbally insulted me in front of all the other students.

My parents had meetings with the school principal about the teacher who had called me a jerk in front of the entire class. My mom was visibly angry at the teacher, and my dad was also frustrated but remained composed. I'm not sure of everything that was said in that meeting. Afterward, I didn't find the teacher to be extremely nice to me, but she never called me a name in front of the entire class again. She also wasn't as aggressive toward me as she had been before the meeting with my parents and the principal.

As I remained courageous and focused on improving my reading, writing, and math skills over the next few years in elementary school, I was able to leave Chapter 1 class and join the other students in regular academic classes. I found myself excelling in music class and was even featured in a local newspaper article for making District Chorus.

I still faced some setbacks in academics that were noticeable to my teachers. At one point, when I was about to graduate from elementary school to middle school, my grammar teacher told me that I might possibly be held back due to my poor handwriting and basic grammar issues. This was devastating news to hear. I had finally joined the rest of my classmates, and now, just as I was about to graduate with them into middle school, the faculty was considering holding me back for another year to repeat my last year of elementary school.

I credit my mom for helping me fix this lingering issue that had been negatively impacting me. She wouldn't let me go outside and play with the other kids in the neighborhood until I finished writing the letters of the alphabet over and over again until my handwriting improved and my homework assignments were completed to one hundred percent.

I was completely done with the handwriting issue. I was finished with teachers telling me that I wasn't meeting their acceptable levels of learning and writing. I was not unintelligent, and I was not slow, as much as one particular teacher and a few peers had projected these traits onto me. Despite the adversity, I accepted the harsh truth that I was behind most of my classmates. I confronted that obstacle head-on.

After some intense focus and lots of neatly writing the same alphabet letters repeatedly, I was able to improve my handwriting and grammar enough to graduate with my friends and classmates. I was ready to move forward to the next level of schooling.

There I found myself—and even better, a new and improved version of myself. I was now a middle school student at Tredyffrin Easttown Middle School in Devon, Pennsylvania. I felt brand new.

Although I faced many challenges and obstacles in elementary school, I learned at a young age that if you want to achieve a goal, you have to be led by courage to get there and cross the finish line. I desperately wanted to be on the same learning level as the other students, and even more desperately, I wanted to graduate elementary school with them. I had to be convinced that I could do it and that I would make it.

In middle school, I not only did well in academics, but surprisingly, I excelled in a few honors and advanced-level classes. Little old me, like the choo-choo train that said, "I think I can, I think I can," had truly captured a strong, individualized learning style that worked solely for me. I think the Chapter 1 classes were actually a blessing in disguise because they taught me personalized learning styles that helped me quickly catch up and excel at advanced levels amongst my peers.

My classmates were all busy with the wide variety of classes, groups, sports, and events that our middle school offered, and I quickly began to progress into some of these areas. I landed a lead role in the annual chorus production as Mr. Bumble in the *Oliver* musical. Me, the kid who had so much trouble reading and writing, was selected to be the morning school announcer, delivering the school announcements over the intercom system broadcast in every classroom.

The icing on the cake, which will forever remain a lifetime achievement for me, was when I was selected as the school's Student of the Month and was published in the local city newspaper. The school held a special ceremony honoring all the Students of the Month that year, and my parents attended. I was so proud of this accomplishment—it brought me immense joy. My parents and I had climbed and overcome so many educational obstacles together.

I became a popular kid in middle school and didn't get into the trouble I occasionally did during elementary school. As I approached my final year of middle school, someone mentioned the upcoming student council elections and the next class president. It was around this time that someone suggested I should run for Student Council President.

In the back of my mind, I thought there was no way a behind-the-curve student from Chapter 1 class—one of the very few African-American students in the entire school—and someone who didn't excel in history, politics, or anything government-related, would win as Student Council President. Fear overwhelmed me and blocked me from entering the nominations.

As usual, when Eddie and Karren, my parents, got wind of this news, they had a field day.

Supportive Mom reminded me of how much my classmates liked me. She reminded me of the time I led the class in changing the school curriculum to better fit our learning standards, which the general students wanted, and the school administration approved the adjustments. She also reminded me of the time I got the school board to approve the first junior high school dance.

She reminded me of the time I rented a ballroom at a hotel for my birthday party, and 95% of my class came to the party that I had planned, paid for, and executed. It was an epic event. My Hollywood celebrity cousin, Tichina Arnold, flew from the West Coast to the East Coast to surprise me at my big-bang birthday bash. When Tichina walked into the ballroom, filled with nearly one hundred kids, their mouths dropped to the floor. She was popular among them from being on the hit *Martin* television show that was freshly airing at the time. Tichina sang the most beautiful and touching rendition of "Happy Birthday" that I had ever heard. As she always does, she elated my heart with her infectious energy, beautiful smile, and angelic voice.

The faces of the other kids at my birthday party were filled with joy and shock, and my mother, of course, had countless snapshots of these priceless moments on her camera. Tichina naturally lights up a room with her joyful spirit, and I, along with those almost one hundred star-struck teenagers, and so many others, were the lucky ones to embrace her love.

My mom told me not to be scared. She encouraged me to use my passion and leadership skills, which I had developed since elementary school, and to run for Student Council President. And so, I did. I won one of the top two spots in the class's voted nominations on the ballot and became a nominee for Student Council President. Things were happening so fast, and here I was, running against a good friend of mine, Dan Ruppe, who was the other top-voted candidate for Student Council President.

My dad, who was very into politics and also a regional manager for Kodak, helped me structure and design my campaign. One of the main campaign slogans we came up with was, "Vote for me, and you will see how much fun things will be." My dad had access to hundreds of colors and varieties of copy paper, and he helped me print hundreds of campaign flyers, postcards, and buttons to distribute my campaign all over the school.

I participated in many speeches and debates. I printed and plastered flyers everywhere in the school. In just a few short months, I had completed my campaign for Student Council President. I couldn't believe that I had found the courage to step out from being the minority, slow-learning boy in Chapter 1 class in elementary school to the nominee for Student Council President in junior high school.

The day finally came when all the students cast their votes for the student council nominees. Mr. Marchiano, the director of the student council, came on the loudspeaker to announce the winners. My heart raced, my hands were sweaty and clammy, and I was more nervous than I had ever been before.

As the winners of each nominated position were announced, from the lowest-ranking position to the top-ranking position—president—I silently and internally agreed with and was happy for most of the winners, but didn't agree with others winning their seats on the Student Council Board.

Finally, after what seemed like the longest announcement of my life, Mr. Marchiano congratulated the winner of the upcoming year's school president... Dan Ruppe, and the runner-up, automatically selected as the Chief Justice Parliamentarian, Karma Butler.

My inner soul trembled, my body slouched in the chair, and I'm sure a few sweltering tears formed behind my eyelids as I absorbed the news that I had lost the long campaign for Student Council President. Looking back on the entire experience years later, I realized that I had exceeded my goals and expectations, even though I didn't win the title.

You see, as Chief Justice Parliamentarian, I was second in command of the student council. Like my father, whom I admired so much for being one of the only Black regional managers in the Philadelphia area with IBM and Kodak, I was the only Black student on the student council board. Not only did I represent the minorities of the school, but I was also the voice of reason, the voice of change, and an activist making a prolific and long-lasting impact on the entire school. Often, to me, it seemed that my responsibilities were far greater than the president's responsibilities.

One day during our year together on the student council, Dan, the elected class president, came to me and said that the school should have voted for me to be president because he saw how hard I constantly worked. He said that he didn't have as much drive and energy as I did. Overall, this notion didn't change the voting results, but my heart melted with gratitude. It created an even stronger working bond between the two of us, and I worked even harder for Dan, my president, as his second in command.

During this experience, I had to not focus on all the issues and concerns weighing on me from my previous learning disabilities, a scornful teacher, pressure from peers, politics, and popularity votes, but rather to look inside myself and choose courage as my guide.

66

"The fears of not being good enough, educated enough, accepted by others, or constantly comparing myself to others were beliefs that held me back from finding my true potential."

The fears of not being good enough, educated enough, accepted by others, or constantly comparing myself to others were beliefs that held me back from finding my true potential. The cruelty—and what I felt to be a form of racism—that was publicly displayed toward me by a teacher in front of my friends and classmates created an almost lifelong stigma. I had built somewhat of a protective and paralyzing bubble around me that, for many years to come, internally isolated me from the outside world in many ways.

Through these challenging times, courage became my friend. Courage was my hero. Courage carried me through the rough seas of darkness to the solid land of brightness on which I currently stand.

Life is about making choices. Make the choice to commit to being courageous in your journey every day—that is my recommendation to you. The alternative is to not be courageous, which will lead you down a path where you remain stagnant, not developing to your full potential, and constantly facing unnecessary struggles, setbacks, and lost opportunities.

You miss 100% of the shots in life that you don't take. You have to choose courage to take the shots in life when they rarely arise. If you choose courage to take those shots and score a win, this is when you can transform your life into amazing achievements, a successful lifestyle, a mindset of fulfillment, and a heart filled with joy.

It will never fail you, and this I know. Choose courage.

Habit 2:
Choose Courage
Steps Toward Choosing Courage

Answer the questions below:

What fear is holding you back from ——————
achieving your biggest goal?

———————————————————————————

———————————————————————————

———————————————————————————

What has made this fear appear ——————
in your present life?

———————————————————————————

———————————————————————————

———————————————————————————

Why do you let this fear create obstacles to
achieving your goal? ——————

———————————————————————————

———————————————————————————

———————————————————————————

Who is making your fear present in your
mind and daily life? _____

_____

_____

What negative words come to mind that best
describe your feelings about your fear? _____

_____

_____

_____

What positive words can you replace for your
negative words about your fear? _____

_____

_____

_____

How can you turn this fear into _____
motivation to achieve your goal?

_____

_____

_____

Fill in and complete the timelines below. Put each week's tasks on your personal calendar.

Week 1

What will you do to overcome our fear this week?

Week 2

What will you do differently from Week 1 to overcome your fear?

Week 3

Choose one person who is close to you and whom you trust to share your fear with.

Who is the person you will share your fear with?

What day of the week will you complete sharing your fear with this person you trust?

Week 4

Share with the same person you trust the steps you have taken during these 4 weeks to overcome your fear. Also, share with them how you feel about your current position in overcoming this fear and putting it behind you.

Chapter 3:

DISCOVER YOUR STRENGTHS AND CREATE ENDLESS OPPORTUNITIES

n elementary school, I participated in a variety of activities, including gymnastics and chorus. I really enjoyed floor tumbling and, even more so, flipping from one bar to another on the uneven bars. However, I didn't enjoy the painful, blood-ripping blisters that covered my entire palms when I didn't use enough powder on the bars.

I remember being in severe pain often during gymnastics. However, our coach taught us that we had to forget about the pain, push through it, and stay focused on showing off our strengths.

One of the gymnasts on our team was a very talented male athlete who was being considered by Olympic coaches to join the U.S.A. Olympic gymnastics team. I remember watching his floor tumbling routines, which were consistently amazing. He performed sequences that included multiple flips, double twists, and triple twists, vaulting high into the sky with every jump, glide, and flip.

I tried to be just as great as he was in gymnastics, but he was always much more skilled, advanced, and naturally talented in the sport. However, I admired his intense focus and abundant talent, and he will always remain an inspiration to me.

Our elementary team didn't compete against other gymnastics teams, but we did perform after-school demonstrations on different gymnastics apparatuses for parents, teachers, and the public. As always, my parents were front and center at every gymnastics demonstration, cheering me on—from the floor routine to the balance beam, the rings, and the uneven bars.

When I progressed to middle school, I continued participating in many activities, including soccer, chorus, and Cub Scouts. Soccer quickly became fascinating to me, and I found that I was very fast on the field, adapting to the sport quickly. I had no background in soccer, but the coach was happy to have me on the team and made me a halfback because I could run quickly while kicking the ball up and down the field, assisting my teammates.

Sometimes, playing in soccer tournaments in the rain was frustrating—sliding and falling in the mud. I strongly disliked getting dirt and grime all over my body, but I knew it was just part of the sport.

Time and time again, I felt like I wasn't a prominent player on the team—I wasn't the one scoring goals or the goalie everyone adored and cheered for. But as I improved my skills, passing the ball to teammates and maneuvering up the field, the coach recognized my aggressiveness in the game. He moved me to an offensive position as a left wing. At that moment, I felt like a much more valuable player, stepping into two different positions as needed—halfback and left wing on offense.

My parents also became favorites among the team. They were one of the few sets of parents who supported the coach by providing snacks and Gatorade during games. They attended every single game, standing front and center on the sidelines, cheering me on. Their presence meant so much to me week after week. Knowing they were always there pushed me to be the best player I could be—not just for myself but for all the fans, family, and friends rooting for our team. They were just as excited as all the players on our team were to win each game—probably even more so.

As time progressed, I became one of the more skilled players on the soccer team, scoring many goals every game. Occasionally, I would step back into the halfback position when the coach needed me to assist the defensive team and the goalie in blocking the opposing team from scoring.

The only real challenge of these tournaments was my asthma. My mom always had to keep my inhaler ready on the sidelines so I could manage my breathing. I was constantly running up and down the field, dribbling the ball, and then rushing to the sideline to take a quick pump from my inhaler before continuing to play. Sometimes, I would score a few goals and then have to run back to the sidelines for another few puffs just to keep my lungs working.

Managing my role as a lead player while keeping up with my asthma routine was difficult at first, but with my parents' support, it eventually became second nature.

There were many times I would be hunched over in the middle of the field, getting ready to score a goal, when my mom would yell from the crowd, "Karma, come get your inhaler! You need to breathe!"

I would yell back from the field, "Mom, I can't right now! We're about to score a goal!"

She would shout back, "Boy, get your butt over here and use this inhaler now!"

Quickly, I would find a moment to sneak away, sprint to the stands where my mom had my inhaler, take a few puffs, and then run right back into the game.

Since I was a premature baby, born two months early, my lungs weren't fully developed, and this caused difficulties year after year throughout my childhood and teenage years. My asthma was triggered by exercise, weather changes, dust, and severe allergies. If the seasons changed too quickly or I caught what, for most people, was just a common cold, I would have an asthma attack—on top of severely battling a cold or flu. I would be admitted to the hospital, staying for one to two weeks on average until I could breathe without an oxygen pump and maintain a normal 90% breathing capacity.

Because I spent so much time in the hospital, I became closely acquainted with the nurses in the children's ward. They became like friends to me. When I was admitted, they would say, "Karma's back!" and greet me warmly. Some even bought me toys and games, and one time, a Nerf basketball hoop to put on the back of my hospital room door.

When my parents visited the hospital, they would often ask where I was—only to find me in the playroom with the nurses instead of resting in my hospital bed. My father, in particular, would get upset and express his frustration, saying, "We came to visit our sick son, and instead, we have to search for him in the playroom?"

Having asthma as a child gave me a deep appreciation for the simple ability to breathe fully. It also taught me profound gratitude and the importance of cherishing fun and exciting moments in life when they came. It often felt like I had to fight just a little harder than others to run and play like a normal kid. There were many times I missed out on trips, celebrations, and special events because I was in the hospital recovering from an asthma attack.

For several years, while intently overcoming the challenges of being asthmatic, I became very skilled at soccer, and I found immense joy in playing the sport. My parents and coach could see my passion for it.

My coach believed I had the potential to advance in the sport, with the ultimate goal of playing professionally. He encouraged my parents to have me try out for the U.S. Youth Soccer team, a stepping stone toward playing at a professional level. We all agreed, and I was beyond excited to compete for a spot on the team.

At the tryouts, I faced some of the most talented and highly recognized youth soccer players in Pennsylvania. I ran harder and competed more intensely than I ever had before, determined to prove I was worthy of a spot on the team.

After the tryouts, I was told that I didn't make the cut for the upcoming season. However, they did acknowledge my skills and placed me on the team's waiting list—meaning if a spot opened, I could potentially be placed on the team.

I was extremely disappointed, but as time passed, I didn't let that setback stop me from learning, growing, and acquiring new skill sets in life.

Several months after that, the season and weather changed drastically, and along with it, I had yet another severe asthma attack. I was hospitalized for my asthma attack, and during my recovery, I had to stay there for what felt like many weeks.

The saddest part of being in the hospital at that time was that I was missing the yearly scheduled Pinewood Derby that my Cub Scouts pack was having. My father and I had designed and built a Pinewood car that we just knew would take one of the top places in the yearly Pinewood Derby competition. We spent so much time crafting the perfect car design for the competition, but my asthma attack unfortunately took over, and I was not able to participate in the Pinewood Derby that year. On top of that, my parents came to visit me at the hospital one day, and they gave me some very gut-wrenching news.

They told me that the coach for the U.S. Youth Soccer team had called them and had offered me a spot on the team that had become available. I had to be available at the time of the call to accept the offer and join the team. Due to my health problems—being in the hospital, recovering from an asthma attack—they had to decline the offer for me to join the U.S. Youth Soccer team.

This news made me very sad, and there in my hospital bed, I cried for a while. I had worked very hard for several years to reach that goal and the opportunity to be on a path as a professional athlete in soccer. My parents always had a special way of communicating with me about how to stay focused on moving forward in life and being the best that I could be while managing the problems and obstacles in my way.

They helped me clearly understand that my ongoing asthma would continue to create obstacles in pursuing the path of becoming a professional athlete in soccer. As much as I had a strong desire to continue playing soccer, I listened to my parents and continued to participate in other sports and activities.

I participated on the track team for a while. The coach found that I was very good at short-distance track running. We also found out that long-distance track running would almost certainly bring on an asthma attack and likely put me in the hospital. We decided to stay away from long-distance events like the mile run.

I was growing as a teenager at the time, and doing so much running caused me to start having knee and shin problems, including severe shin splints. The ice bag routine—15 minutes on my legs, 15 minutes off—before and after track meets became its own program that wasn't very enjoyable, in addition to the actual strenuous track meets themselves, especially on my lungs.

I learned that I was very good at handing off a baton to my teammates and winning short-distance events. I also learned that jumping hurdles wasn't for me, as I constantly clipped the hurdle and fell painfully to the ground on my hands and knees. Repeatedly, I knocked the hurdles down instead of jumping over them. All of this put together led to a quick end to my time on the track team.

Up to this point, I had always been a member of the church choir, singing solos that were often requested by my pastor, Dr. Pollard, of Zion Baptist Church in Ardmore, Pennsylvania. The Christmas season, in particular, was extremely fun when I got to sing "White Christmas" as a duet at the church, performing alongside my mother, Karren.

Singing at the church brought me so much joy that I decided to audition for my school chorus. The chorus director, Carmen E. Culp, was an extraordinary musical director and highly respected in the music profession as a publisher, author, and professor. Mrs. Culp believed that I had a great voice that needed coaching, training, and development, and she accepted me into the school chorus.

Mrs. Culp was one of those serious and focused teachers you just didn't mess around with. When she said "stand," you stood up as tall as you could, like a soldier. When she said "sing," you sang from your diaphragm with all your might. When she said "jump," you better jump like your life depended on it—otherwise, there would be problems, and you did not want problems with Mrs. Culp.

Mrs. Culp took a strong liking to my performance talents and to me. She taught me very important speaking and performance skills, such as how to properly hold a microphone, how to enunciate with diction, how to project, and how to breathe properly by using my diaphragm.

During one of her greatest masterpieces produced for the school—the Broadway musical *Oliver Twist*—she cast me in the lead role of Mr. Bumble. It became very challenging for me during rehearsals. On top of normal classroom studies and homework, as the lead in the musical, I had a lot of scripts and scenes to memorize. This was the first time I had a role as a lead actor and singer in a musical. I felt that I was better at and enjoyed the singing part of the role, but based on the laughter from the audience during performances, I think I did pretty well with the acting part too.

The years went by, and I was about to move on to high school. Mrs. Culp took a serious interest in guiding my future development in the performing arts. She told my parents that one of the best performing arts schools in the United States for high school students was in Virginia—the Governor's School for the Arts.

My parents and I researched the school's history and found that its graduates had gone on to prominent careers in the arts, Broadway, and various fields of the entertainment industry.

We had to travel from Philadelphia to Virginia to audition at the school in order to be accepted. The school had five different departments, and I didn't know which one to audition for. I chose to audition for the Theatre Department, the Vocal Music Department, and the Performing Arts Department.

For several months, I prepared monologues and songs for the audition in Virginia. My parents did a lot of planning for the trip, and we traveled to Virginia, where I auditioned for three of the five departments at the Governor's School for the Arts.

The vocal music audition wasn't too bad, but I did hear a lot of classical opera-style singers performing in front of me, and I was *not* Mr. Opera.

The Theatre Department was a bit intimidating, and my nerves really kicked in because it was just me performing my monologue in front of a panel of teachers. The head chairman of the department was giving me a serious look with a straight face the entire time I performed my monologue.

The Performing Arts Department audition was the most stressful and nerve-racking because I had to sing a solo, perform a monologue, and then dance with a group of dancers to choreography they taught us. To say that I was a horrible dancer compared to the others—who, to me, moved like Mikhail Baryshnikov's protégés—would be an understatement.

After the stressful and emotionally draining auditions, my parents and I returned home to the suburbs of Philadelphia, where I waited for a few weeks for the results.

I was extremely worried that I wouldn't get into the school in any department based on my perception of the tremendous talent pool I saw at every audition.

I was in complete shock when my parents told me that not only had I been *accepted* into the school, but I had been accepted into every department I had auditioned for. I simply couldn't believe it.

Now, I had tremendous pressure to choose the department that would lay the foundation for my performing arts education and career. I didn't know which one to choose, but I knew that the Performing Arts Department combined singing, dancing, and acting into one program.

After considering the benefits of each department, my parents and I decided on the Performing Arts Department. We formally accepted the invitation, and I was set to start my first year of high school in Virginia. The only problem was that we had to be residents of one of seven Hampton Roads cities in Virginia—but we lived in the suburbs of Philadelphia, Pennsylvania.

My always-incredible parents came up with a plan. Within a few months, we sold our home in Pennsylvania and moved to Virginia. By August, I was registered at Great Bridge High School in Chesapeake, Virginia, for my required academic classes and at the Governor's School for the Arts for my performing arts major.

How my parents managed to pull this off—paying for two houses at once until the Pennsylvania home sold—is still a mystery to me, and I am forever grateful for their strength and dedication to achieving my goals and dreams.

I don't have any children of my own yet, but my parents, Karren and Eddie, have definitely taught me—by leading by example—how to go above and beyond in supporting your kids' goals and dreams in life. I am eternally grateful that they made such a grand gesture for me because what I didn't know at the time was that attending the Governor's School for the Arts would be one of the most life-changing, wonderful, impactful, and guiding experiences that would lay the foundation for my adult life and career opportunities.

That summer was so much fun as I began rehearsals every day at Chrysler Hall in Norfolk, Virginia—the largest performance venue for concerts, tours, and Broadway shows in the city. This is where the Performing Arts Department held summer rehearsals for the traveling performances it produced before the school year curriculum started.

Directed by the Chairman of the Performing Arts Department, Chip Gallagher, and choreographed by the department's choreographer, Jeff Warner, we were putting together a collection of top hit pop songs from the '60s to the '90s. "I Want You Back" by Michael Jackson, "Love Keeps Lifting Me Higher" by Jackie Wilson, and "Do You Love Me" by The Contours were a few of the songs in the medley.

Every day, I was surrounded by some of the most talented high school singers and dancers in the Hampton Roads area of Virginia. One day during rehearsal, I was a chorus singer staged in the back row of the scene we were practicing. The director, Chip, noticed me and said that I had a great smile and needed to be in the front of the group on stage. From that experience, I learned the power and magic of a genuine and authentic smile.

I caught on pretty quickly to the skill of singing and moving around the stage with minimal choreography while holding a microphone. However, I did not catch on quickly at all to the advanced, synchronized dance choreography performed by the main dancers—who were often at the front of the stage, where I had been placed because of my smile.

In fact, I became the center of jokes among the top dancers because I often tripped over my own two feet. Some even requested that the director and choreographer not place them near me on stage because I had "fly swatter" arms and hands, constantly hitting and bumping into the other performers.

When school began in September, it was challenging to get used to attending two separate high schools every day. Within several months, I adapted to going to Great Bridge High School for academics in the morning and then to the Governor's School for the Arts in the afternoon.

It was a requirement of attending the Governor's School for the Arts that I maintain a grade of "C" or above in my academic high school classes at Great Bridge High School. The city of Chesapeake, where Great Bridge High School was located, and the Governor's School for the Arts together paid my yearly tuition to attend the performing arts school. I worked really hard every day to do well on my homework assignments and tests, always making sure to maintain "A" grades because I didn't want to get kicked out of the Governor's School for the Arts—it was my joy, my passion, and my love every day.

Several evenings each week, we continued to have rehearsals for our shows at the performing arts department. Our productions were top-tier, and we were held to a professional standard, even though we were high school students. We were taught, directed, and produced by professionals who were Broadway stars, theater icons, music industry moguls, and television and film actors. Our shows traveled to schools, concert halls, and performance venues throughout the seven Hampton Roads cities and several surrounding states.

We even toured Japan, performing in four different cities, where we were treated like Hollywood celebrities. In Japan, we performed in Osaka, Kitakyushu, Hiroshima, and Miyazaki. Concert fans surrounded our tour bus, flooded our dressing rooms backstage, and screamed and cheered as if we were Taylor Swift. We had never experienced anything like this before, even after performing the same show numerous times in America. A few of the Japanese fans even followed us to every city where we performed.

Touring Japan with our performance group, *The Voices of Virginia*, as a young teenager was a life-changing and unforgettable experience that I'm sure all of us in the group will cherish forever.

Besides enjoying the experience of being a performer in Japan, I gained a deep appreciation for basic commodities that we often take for granted in America.

In Japan, I personally experienced how water is not wasted but rather shared and used multiple times for different purposes. Some toilets had sinks built on top of them, and families shared reused bathwater to soak in after showering separately to conserve water.

Homes and hotels in Japan were typically compact, with small living spaces and twin-sized mattresses or floor mats for sleeping. In one of the cities we toured, I encountered toilets that resembled urinals on a wall—but instead of sitting, you had to squat over the urinal-like hole to use the restroom.

In several of the cities we toured, *The Voices of Virginia* stayed with homestay families. I learned firsthand about the strong sense of unity in Japanese family living, where multiple generations—including children, parents, and grandparents—live under one roof.

One concept that fascinated me was that during the school day, Japanese students were released to go home for lunch. Instead of eating in a cafeteria, they enjoyed a home-cooked meal with their family. This was completely different from the American school lunch routine I was used to, where hundreds of students piled into a packed cafeteria to quickly scarf down what often resembled packaged fast food.

Japanese culture also places a huge emphasis on respect—people bow when they greet each other, especially when showing respect to elders. I also noticed that Japanese youth are taught significant responsibilities at a young age, both at home and at school. At school, students were responsible for the general upkeep and janitorial duties of the building.

Traveling to Japan as a young teenager was one of the best experiences of my life. It opened my eyes to an entire world beyond my personal experiences, vision, and beliefs. I realized that "I don't know what I don't know." After spending two weeks in Japan, it became clear to me that living the same daily routine within the same culture could limit my personal growth and opportunities in the world.

When I returned to America, and as my next three years at the Governor's School for the Arts progressed, I became a much better singer—often landing solos—and, surprisingly, a much better dancer. I worked hard to improve my dancing skills so much that by the time I was about to graduate, my dance abilities had become so advanced that the Performing Arts Department sent me to the Dance Department for additional training.

I also took on a leadership role as the first-ever production manager for our tour group, a position offered to me by our chairman, Chip. I was responsible for managing the performers, stage sets, equipment, venue operations, and tour logistics. I even created and became president of our parent-student organization, ensuring that teachers, parents, and students worked together to achieve the same goals.

As president, I served as the liaison between teachers, parents, and students—representing the needs and requests of the Performing Arts Department students. I planned, coordinated, and executed the department's first trip to Broadway in New York City, which included about forty students, teachers, and chaperones.

My ever-supportive mom was an executive board member of the parent-student organization. She didn't like me calling her "Mrs. Butler" during meetings for the official record. One day, in front of all the board members, she looked directly at me and said, "Please don't call me Mrs. Butler—call me Mom."

I explained that the secretary couldn't write "Mom" in the official meeting minutes that were distributed to the department and that her name had to appear as "Mrs. Butler." She was not happy about this and made sure I knew it with her silent glare across the table. However, to support the structure of the meeting, and since other parents were around, she reluctantly went along with it—*barely*.

Wanting to make an impact at Great Bridge High School as well, I proposed a student showcase to the principal for Black History Month, featuring performances of songs by legendary Black artists like The Supremes and Stevie Wonder. The principal approved my proposal, and I held auditions, cast talented singers and dancers, and successfully produced the show for the entire student body.

We rehearsed a thirty- to forty-five-minute performance for several weeks. I would attend Great Bridge High School from 7 AM to 12 PM and then go to the Governor's School for the Arts from 2 PM to 5 PM. After that, I would travel back to Great Bridge High School for rehearsals of the Black History Show that I was producing from 6 PM to 8 PM.

One day, my body made it very clear that I was overexerting myself with my extremely long and physically exhausting daily schedule. During rehearsals one night at Great Bridge High School, I was teaching choreography to the performers when I suddenly collapsed to the ground. I tried to stand back up, but I couldn't—my legs were cramping and in severe pain. I ate a lot of bananas to increase my low potassium levels, drank a lot of electrolytes, and took it easy during rehearsals for the next few days. My legs became stronger, and I recovered.

My dad was extremely worried about me—and upset with me at the same time. He told me that I couldn't schedule myself to do so many things every day and expect my body to perform at 100%. By then, I was already committed to my two high schools, *The Voices of Virginia* traveling shows, and producing the Black History Show, so I couldn't back out. However, I did make an effort moving forward to avoid over-scheduling myself every day.

In February that year at Great Bridge High School, we performed the first-ever Black History Show. We held several performances so that all of the students in the school had the chance to see it. The show was very well received by both students and staff, and my popularity at the school increased. Since I was usually only there in the mornings, I hadn't had the chance to get to know a large portion of the student body.

Later that year, Great Bridge High School presented me with an award for producing the show. I was deeply touched and grateful for the recognition.

It was a true honor and pleasure to be a part of two high schools at the same time, to perform in shows that traveled the country and the world, and to become an impactful leader in various ways for the students and faculty of the Governor's School for the Arts and Great Bridge High School.

After going through so many course changes and disappointments in soccer, track, and gymnastics, I had finally found the spark that inspired me—the performing arts. Day in and day out, I was energized and driven to excel in this field. It was profoundly because of my parents and the incredible, life-changing programs at the Governor's School for the Arts that I was able to do exactly that.

Graduation from my two high schools was a very busy time, but it was also filled with highly rewarding achievements that I had earned throughout my four-year journey.

I thankfully graduated from Great Bridge High School ranked in the top thirty of my graduating class. I was surprised to receive the President's Academic Achievement Award, several partial college scholarships, and to be featured in the national publication *Who's Who Among American High School Students*.

The honor that meant the most to me was being voted Most Talented Male and Most Likely to Succeed by my graduating class for the yearbook superlatives. However, the yearbook committee made me choose one, so I selected *Most Talented Male*.

At my graduation from the Governor's School for the Arts, I was honored as a Valedictorian of the Performing Arts Department. I received multiple awards and opportunities as a result of this prestigious title. The *Virginian-Pilot*, our local newspaper, even featured me on the front page of a section celebrating me as a graduating valedictorian, with the title of the article *"Head of the Class"* alongside my senior outdoor photo.

It was all happening so fast, and it was incredibly exciting. A journalist from the newspaper came to our house and interviewed me and my parents. In the published article, the journalist recounted a time when my parents attended my first singing performance at church, expecting to get a good laugh—but instead, they were shocked to discover that I was actually a good singer.

I was given the incredible honor of being a speaker at the Governor's School for the Arts commencement ceremony as a valedictorian graduate. During the ceremony, I was surprised to be presented with the Dartmouth College Book Award for outstanding leadership in the performing arts.

Ironically, I received a scholarship to the California Institute of the Arts to major in dance. Imagine that—the same freshman who tripped over his own two feet, the one other performers didn't want to be on stage with because I would accidentally run into them or hit them—was now a college dance major on scholarship!

As if my schedule wasn't already packed with excitement, I was preparing to move across the country to California for college when I received some last-minute, exciting—and not-so-exciting—news.

I was originally supposed to head to Japan for my second tour with *The Voices of Virginia*, but I was contacted by Paramount Parks and offered a contract as a main stage dancer for the summer. Several months earlier, I had auditioned for Paramount Parks but didn't book the job and was placed on a standby waiting list—similar to my experience with the U.S. Youth Soccer Team tryouts.

I made the difficult decision to turn down the opportunity to perform in Japan for a second time in order to accept my first professional dance contract with a major entertainment company. Just a few days after graduation, I moved to Richmond, Virginia, to work for Paramount Parks at their King's Dominion location.

The job paid very well, and I had the opportunity to work with the famed choreographer Barry Lather, who was known for choreographing for celebrities and movies like *The Blues Brothers*. Learning his hip-hop choreography was challenging for me at first, but after weeks of rehearsals and performing the show up to five times a day on the main stage, I quickly adapted to hip-hop dance.

The cast of professional performers at Paramount Parks was among the most talented singers, dancers, and actors I had ever worked with. Many of them had careers in television, Broadway, national tours, and cruise ships. They became like family to me, and many of them remained close friends that I would continue to work with and hang out with in Los Angeles.

At the end of one of the most exciting summers of my life, I moved to Valencia, California—just north of Los Angeles—to attend the California Institute of the Arts as a dance major on a scholarship. It was a complete turnaround from four years earlier when I had been the worst dancer on stage, teased by other performers for my lack of coordination. Now, I was a college dance major and a working professional performer.

To this day, these stories and experiences remain a testament to victory and triumph in my life. My hope for you is that you stay focused on improving yourself while facing and overcoming the challenges, roadblocks, and obstacles that life throws your way.

66

"...it is crucial to fill your subconscious with the belief that you are a winner, that you *will* achieve your dreams, and that you are *beautiful just the way you are.*"

You *must* believe in yourself. Your subconscious mind doesn't know the difference between what is real and what is imagined. It is constantly searching for ways to fulfill whatever thoughts you feed it. That's why it is crucial to fill your subconscious with the belief that you are a winner, that you *will* achieve your dreams, and that you are *beautiful just the way you are.*

If you don't do this, your subconscious will easily fulfill the negative thoughts you repeatedly tell yourself, leading to failure, fear, doubt, and even insanity.

This is the first vital step in believing in yourself—one that many people miss—but it is completely achievable if you have the understanding, vision, motivation, and dedication to nurture your thoughts and work toward your goals and dreams.

Although the entire cast had moved on from the Black History Show at Great Bridge High School nearly twenty years earlier, one of the lead singers, Kimberly Clark, contacted my mother years later on Facebook.

She told my mother that she had been following my entrepreneurship on social media over the years and wanted to express her gratitude for the impact I had on her life. She mentioned how much time, energy, and care I had put into producing the Black History Show and how it remained a forever-memorable and inspiring experience for her.

Hearing this made me stop and think—Wow. Something I had produced nearly two decades ago had left such a lasting impact on someone that they felt compelled to reach out and express their appreciation. Kim's gesture of gratitude and support, even decades later, truly meant the world to me.

Kim's thoughtfulness in reaching out to me through my mother reminded me to continue letting the spark inside of me shine and inspire others to live their best lives. You never know what someone else has or doesn't have, or what they are or aren't going through. You personally can be the single most inspiring factor that changes the course of someone's moment, day, week, or even life for the better.

Over the years, as an adult riding the roller coaster of life—as we all do—I achieved many incredible successes. I became a managing partner and owner with Texas Roadhouse, America's #1-rated steakhouse chain. I was featured worldwide as a recording artist by a division of Sony and, surprisingly, reached #1 on their music chart. I became an executive producer of a television series I created, which aired on affiliates of CBS and My Network TV. I even achieved my long-sought personal goal of earning a six-figure income each year.

But completely opposite to these successes—despite being a purposeful, positive, encouraging, and spirited person—I faced life-changing experiences. I battled such severe depression that I became homeless and almost lost my life.

I was hospitalized and then placed in a behavioral health treatment center to overcome the internal struggles of depression that had blocked me from achieving and winning in my daily path of life.

After this significant, eye-opening experience, I learned that life can flip upside down in the blink of an eye if you let it. Never give up on yourself, your hopes, your dreams, or the people and things that matter most to you. I endured a brutal life lesson and paid a significant price in loss, character, and time—one that I never want you to experience. Please learn from my mistakes and downfalls so that you can be all that you're meant to be and more.

After battling severe depression, I spent several years purposely rebuilding my courage, strengthening my spirit, and nurturing my calling to be of service to others. During this time of focused reinvigoration, I was profoundly guided and supported by my angel—my mother.

From these experiences, I now better understand what is truly important in my life, and at the top of that list is making a difference.

When you make a difference, you cause change that has a significant effect on people and their situations. Unlike fame and fortune—which many seek—the intent and follow-through to positively impact someone's life, whether you know them or not, provides endless benefits.

This intent to make a difference brings long-term fulfillment, expands your personal growth, propels your daily joy, and ultimately serves as a secret weapon that you can use repeatedly to make your life purposeful, rewarding, and deeply enjoyable.

When you acknowledge the limited time you have on Earth, you begin to recognize the things you truly want to accomplish and the people with whom you want to spend your time. I strongly encourage you to focus on completing those things that matter most to you and positively impacting the lives of those around you.

By making a difference, your life will become abundantly filled with satisfaction, achievement, and love—the very things you and the world need.

Find the spark and the light that illuminates you. Figure out how to make your light shine as brightly as possible, and share it with the world. Dive limitless into your life with purpose. Make a difference.

Habit 3:

Make a Difference

Steps to Make a Difference

Identify three activities that you enjoy doing in your personal time.

- _____

_____

- _____

_____

- _____

_____

Which one of the above activities do you think is most beneficial to the people in and around your community?

_____

_____

_____

What are three tasks you can complete to
further develop your skills in the activity you
chose above?

- _____

- _____

- _____

What are three ways you can use these
skills to help others?

- _____

- _____

- _____

List three people whose lives you want to make a positive impact on:

- _____
  _____

- _____
  _____

- _____
  _____

Chapter 4:

EXPLORE MANY GEMS TO GET YOUR BRIGHT SHINING DIAMOND

A fter graduating high school, a few months later, I moved to beautiful California. Living in the sun and having fun, I settled in Hollywood with my best friend from college, Jennifer, and briefly with my cousin Tichina in Los Angeles.

During this exciting time—transitioning from my teenage years to my twenties—I was motivated and driven to pursue a career as a professional singer, dancer, and actor. My roommate Jennifer worked at a talent agency in Los Angeles and recommended me to her boss as a potential talent. Thanks to Jennifer's recommendation, Steve, the agency owner, agreed to represent me. This opened the door for casting opportunities in lead roles for upcoming television shows, music videos, and national commercials.

During the day, I would go from one audition to the next. In the evenings, I attended acting classes with a famous Hollywood coach, Richard Brander, and then repeated the cycle, usually Monday through Friday.

Not only was this routine mentally and physically exhausting, but it also didn't provide for life's essentials—clothes, food, or rent. To make ends meet, I followed a friend's suggestion and signed up for Central Casting Los Angeles.

Central Casting Los Angeles is the largest and most well-known company for casting background extras in television and film. Calling their hotline every day felt like dialing a random 1-800 number. When I finally got through to a live person, they would ask about my physical features—skin color, height, and the like. These questions didn't feel very personal, but it was a necessary step that I, along with thousands of other aspiring extras, had to take daily to book gigs.

Eventually, I started landing occasional background roles through Central Casting in major motion pictures and television shows. After weeks and months of persistence, casting agents began calling me directly for jobs.

I earned Screen Actors Guild credits for appearing as a background extra in movies like *American Pie and Bowfinger*. I also had tremendous fun working on television shows such as *Beverly Hills, 90210, Sister, Sister, and Clueless*.

While working on *Clueless*, I had a memorable moment during a break when Stacey Dash, one of my celebrity icons, approached me. I was lying on a lawn chair next to a pool when she struck up a conversation. My heart raced, and my hands were sweaty with nervousness—it was surreal that out of all the actors on set, she chose to talk to me. I'll never forget that day.

Booking background roles soon became my primary source of income. While meeting celebrities and working on set was exciting, it also had its downsides. Often, I felt like just a prop or tool. The most challenging part was the conflict of interest these jobs created with my talent manager.

Steve had been booking me for auditions for major television and film roles. These opportunities were thrilling, as they involved competing with some of Hollywood's top stars. However, these auditions consumed most of my time and didn't pay. The one exception was a *Bowfinger* union audition, which compensated me for my time.

Eddie Murphy starred in *Bowfinger*, and while I didn't meet him personally, I was near him in several scenes. Even though I can't spot myself in the final cut of the film, it was still an incredible experience. The paycheck from the union audition was a lifeline—it allowed me to pay rent to my roommate, Jennifer, who was strict about timely payments. At the time, the check felt monumental.

At the height of my collaboration with my manager Steve, he secured a final casting call for a lead role in *G's Trippin*. I was one of three finalists, competing against Donald Faison for the part. Around the same time, I was offered a large recurring feature role as a background extra on a television series through the background casting agency.

When I informed Steve about the double booking, he was furious. He insisted that his auditions took priority, stating that real actors in Hollywood didn't do extra work. I ultimately chose the audition for the major motion picture, not wanting to jeopardize my relationship with Steve. Unfortunately, I didn't land the role after the final screen test.

I was heartbroken. Not only had I missed out on the lead role, but I also passed up a high-paying extra gig and had no money to pay my bills. Despite the setbacks, I remained determined. I added a commercial agent and a dance agent to assist in achieving my goals.

My commercial agent sent me to auditions for national brands like State Farm and AT&T. Meanwhile, my dance agent, DDO Artists Agency, represented me at the top level of the dance industry. I made callbacks for

Janet Jackson's *Velvet Rope* Tour and Prince's MTV Awards performance, but I didn't book either. The injuries I sustained while dancing at these auditions, combined with the constant grind, left me physically and emotionally drained.

After moving from Los Angeles back to my hometown in Virginia, I pushed myself to find my greatness through my passions and produced my television series, *American Dance Legend*.

I sought support from people within my community. I received assistance from the performing arts school I attended for four years, The Governor's School for the Arts, as well as from Todd Rosenlieb Dance, where I worked as a dance teacher. Even with this profound assistance, I was still missing some key components for a television show, including a director, cinematographers, sound and lighting teams, and a broadcast spot on television.

At the time, I was performing on the live broadcast of the Miss Virginia competition, acting as a singer, dancer, and host—or, as we were called, a "Miss Virginia Man." Our primary job was to support the contestants and make them look great on stage and on camera as they competed for the title of Miss Virginia, with one advancing to Miss America. One year, during this show, I had the opportunity to co-perform with Caressa Cameron, who later became Miss America.

During breaks in rehearsals and recordings for the live Miss Virginia production, I would often wander backstage and around the venue, meeting the production team, lighting crew, and sound crew. I was fascinated by the enormous satellite bus parked behind the venue, typically used for live news and sports broadcasts. One day, the side door of the bus was open, and I couldn't resist peeking inside. The bus was filled with monitors, lights, soundboards, and an array of intricate gadgets.

Inside the bus, I saw a tall gentleman whom I recognized as the live television broadcast director of the show. He had been working with us all week during rehearsals. I asked if I could come in and look around, and he graciously allowed me to enter. He explained how the monitors, producers, directors, and satellites work together to send a live signal to broadcast stations for airing live events.

I distinctly remember the excitement of learning this "magical" new skill set, which captivated me and left me wanting more. As our conversation continued, I shared that I was trying to produce my own television show but lacked training as a producer and didn't have access to a production crew.

To my surprise, he mentioned that he was from the same town as I was and worked full-time as a producer for a major news network. He explained that he had access to camera crews, sound and lighting equipment, and resources for independent television productions. I was thrilled that I had stepped away from the usual off-stage camaraderie with cast members and taken the initiative to explore and connect with the crew.

He suggested that I schedule a meeting with him after the current production, and I did just that. It felt like the angels had answered my prayers.

Meeting him back in our hometown at the news station office marked the beginning of a dream coming to life. Together, we finalized the production schedule and recordings for my first television show as an executive producer. The show was called *Fever*.

Before filming, I reached out to an advertising agency I had worked with previously. The agency owner, John, told me he had purchased broadcast spots on several local channels through his company, Tele-Video Productions, and could air my television show. I couldn't believe how everything was coming together.

I went full speed ahead, holding casting auditions at schools and performing arts centers across the Hampton Roads area. One audition was held at The Governor's School for the Arts in Norfolk, Virginia. It was an honor to work with talented singers, dancers, and actors auditioning for the show or featuring in commercial spots.

The recording of *Fever* took place in front of a live studio audience at a venue located at the Governor's School for the Arts, where I also taught as a performing arts teacher. The experience was euphoric—I had come full circle. I will always be grateful to the Governor's School for the Arts for their unwavering support and the life-changing opportunities they provided, including hosting my television show.

Instead of feeling anxiety, stress, or discomfort as a new executive producer leading a production team, cast, and live audience shoots, I felt an overwhelming sense of comfort. I was filled with excitement, happiness, and bliss as I watched the cast and audience enjoy themselves. *Fever* was broadcast on a local television network, reaching the seven cities of Hampton Roads, Virginia, and was well received.

After the show aired, I reflected on my journey. For years, I had auditioned tirelessly to be part of someone else's show. Now, with the support of my community and talented performers, I had created a platform for young artists to showcase their talents on television. Producing *Fever* was one of the most fulfilling experiences of my life, and I craved more of that joy.

Since then, I've continued to pursue my passion, executive producing three seasons of *American Dance Legend,* two of which aired on CBS and My Network TV affiliates.

The joy I found wasn't about being on television or having my own show. It came from helping others achieve their dreams and uniting communities through passion, vision, and the performing arts.

"

"Fill your thoughts with creativity, positivity, and new ideas that bring you fulfillment, excitement, and joy."

Though the journey was challenging, it was worth every second to find my greatness. I had to take a leap of faith, venture into unfamiliar territory, work harder than ever before, and trust myself.

When situations became difficult, and I wanted to quit—and there were many of those moments—I chose to persevere. I stood up for my team, my cast, and my community. Together, we achieved incredible dreams. I found my greatness.

I encourage you to stand up for what you believe in and for those you believe in. When you dedicate your time, energy, and efforts to helping others achieve their goals, something magical happens—a united force of greatness naturally emerges.

Take time to acknowledge what excites you, motivates you, and sparks your curiosity. What may seem like a faint glimpse of inspiration could turn out to be the most wonderful accomplishment of your life—something you've brought into reality. Your reality is shaped by your thought patterns transformed into actions. Fill your thoughts with creativity, positivity, and new ideas that bring you fulfillment, excitement, and joy. This is how you will discover your greatness.

Start by taking a leap of faith today. Stop waiting for tomorrow—because tomorrow may not come. Find your greatness.

Habit 4:

Find Your Greatness

Steps to Find Your Greatness

Identify What You Are Good At and Your Strongest Abilities

Write three things you are good at:

- _____
  _____

- _____
  _____

- _____
  _____

Use Your Time to Serve Others

Write three acts of service you want to complete in the near future or ways you have recently helped someone achieve a personal goal or serve others:

- _____

- _____

-

Try Different Activities, Hobbies, and Experiences

Write three new activities you want to try in the near future or that you have recently done:

-

-

-

Visit a Variety of Places

Write three new places you want to visit in the near future or that you have recently been to:

-

-

• _____

_____

Identify People You Admire the Most

Write three names of people you admire whether you know them personally or not and the qualities that inspire you:

Name of person you admire _____

Qualities you admire _____

_____

_____

_____

Name of person you admire _____

Qualities you admire _____

_____

_____

Name of person you admire ⸻⸻⸻⸻⸻

Qualities you admire ⸻⸻⸻⸻⸻⸻⸻

_____

_____

_____

Surround Yourself with Successful and Genuinely Good People, Then Model Them.

Name three people who currently surround you or whom you want to surround yourself with, and describe what makes them successful or genuinely good people:

Name of successful/genuinely good person

_____

Their successes and good traits ⸻⸻⸻⸻

_____

_____

_____

Name of successful/genuinely good person

Their successes and good traits ———————

Name of successful/genuinely good person

Their successes and good traits ———————

Chapter 5:

UNCOVER THE HIDDEN YOU

During the fall season of 2018, I boldly made an intentional decision to do something different with my life. Owning and operating restaurants was an incredible twenty-one-year journey. The quest to tap into what was really bothering my inner core finally nagged at me enough for me to take action.

Motivating others has always been a delight of mine. During my weekly manager meetings at my restaurant, I always wanted to do more than just preach sales numbers, food cost, profitability, and guest counts. I wanted to connect with the leaders in my management team on a level that positively impacted their growth and the development of both their personal and professional goals.

To make these purposeful tasks come to life, before every weekly manager meeting, I would research inspiring topics that I thought would help my management team unite, grow, and excel. At every meeting, I included time for each manager to share their weekly progress in their personal and professional development plans. Throughout the meeting, I shared motivational videos that were intended to inspire, spark action, and drive solutions.

As a restaurateur, I learned that the way to someone's heart and soul is through their stomach. I've grown a strong passion for feeding people amazing meals. I would feed my management team lunch from a different restaurant every week during the meetings to show my genuine appreciation for their daily dedication and efforts to lead our team.

The combination of creative meeting agendas, soul-satisfying food, and personalized, inspiring motivation was a magical package that I created week after week, and I loved it. The management team of about 15 showed up on time, week after week, for the meetings, and this was our time to grow together.

One particular day, after the final motivational video was shared at the end of the meeting, one of the managers approached me. He took his time to share with me that I was extremely passionate about the motivational section of the meeting and that I should consider becoming a motivational speaker. I thanked him for his kind words of encouragement as I stood there in the role as the Managing Partner of the restaurant. I did not give his thoughtful communication validation, and I inconsiderately continued forward with my packed work schedule.

Very soon after, I reflected on that conversation about becoming a motivational speaker. Over time, this thought and interest repeatedly captured my attention. Soon, the idea became a constant presence in my mind, and I found myself studying and researching how to become a motivational speaker.

It became such a driving force for my life that I found myself stepping out of my long-lived restaurant career that meant everything to me, and more. My restaurant career was on a path to unimaginable heights. Emerging into the fields of self-development and motivational speaking at the time seemed very risky. The experience was like taking a hike on some random new trail.

Me: "Hey, Mom, I'm going to be a motivational speaker."

Mom: "Karma, how are you going to motivate people if you're so depressed?"

At the time, I didn't realize how depressed I really was, but my mom, unfortunately, was looking at the weak, falling, and failing version of myself that was burning in flames right in front of her—and I knew it.

I had the vision of greatness. I had the vision to be of service to others, but at the time, I didn't have the focus, strength, or courage to make any of my aspirations come true. I knew that I had to quickly pivot and make tough decisions if I truly wanted to rebound, succeed, and win.

I made the tough decision to realize that I deserved happiness in a relationship, and that the current seven-year relationship I was in was draining and toxic. I had to move forward alone, even if it was heartbreaking and gut-wrenching.

I made the tough decision to let go of the dream house I was living in, a place I had worked so hard for. I had my dream large in-ground pool in my backyard, covered by a fully enclosed gazebo. The pool was alongside a lake in my dream neighborhood in a gated, private Orlando community with the most beautiful and comforting views.

After starting a new chapter of life alone, I downsized to a luxury apartment in a resort-style complex. Just when I thought things were getting better, they became even worse. Financially, I couldn't afford the upscale lifestyle I was used to living, and I had to move out of my apartment. I had nowhere to go, and I had run out of the savings, stocks, and funds I had acquired from many years of being on salary in my career.

I stayed in hotels as long as I could. I moved to a different hotel with the best rate I could find online about every other day. In Orlando, during the off-season, there were plenty of four-star hotels to choose from. It became a grueling nightly process to look for the next "hot deal," which literally took hours to research and book. It was mentally draining, and this repeated process made me feel like a failure day after day. But I had to find the next place to move to, almost every day, just to have a roof over my head.

66

"When I finally made the decision to confront my reality, forgive myself, acknowledge myself, dream bigger, and dive deeper, everything began to change for the better."

This went on for several weeks. When I couldn't get a hotel because of busy weekends booked by out-of-town travelers, I would sleep in my car in the parking lot of a hotel that I felt somewhat safe at. I never shared with my mom that I was sometimes sleeping in my car, but somehow, I think her motherly instinct knew. Soon, my angel—my mom—surprised me by flying in from the opposite side of the country, from her home in Las Vegas to me in Orlando.

My supportive mother not only came to be with me during my toughest time of not having a home to live in, but she also went above and beyond by paying for several nights of my hotel stays and stayed with me in the hotel. I can't begin to tell you how much it meant to me that during my darkest moments, my mom was by my side, going through the pain, embarrassment, and my lowest moments with me together.

A family of a close friend found out about me living in hotels and my car and let me stay in their guest living space connected to their home. I was living on the mercy of a wing and a prayer every day, and still, my lifestyle continued to crumble to pieces because I chose to give up.

An unfortunate chain of events continued to arise. However, I had a roof over my head, which meant the world to me, thanks to a loving and supportive friend and their family. I had secured a high-paying job at a premier furniture outlet that had opened in Orlando, but I was so far behind on paying my bills that my car was repossessed. Yet again, although I thought I was on the road to winning, I felt like the biggest failure in life— and now, I had no car for transportation.

I couldn't cry anymore. I couldn't beat myself up anymore. I couldn't dwell on the past anymore. I realized I was my own problem, my own enemy, self-sabotaging myself, and this was when I stopped being a victim. I stopped blaming the world, and I stopped beating myself up. I began to dive deeply and rebound.

I made the tough decision to come to peace with my car, which was ninety percent paid off, being repossessed during a chain of events where I was steadily falling. I was now relying on rides from people that I knew, as well as the Orlando public transportation system.

I made the tough decision to be at peace with my bold decision to step away from my twenty-one-year career, with massive success, in the restaurant industry.

I made the tough decision to acknowledge that I had given up on myself, on everything that was important to me, on everyone I knew, and on everything I had achieved. I was beyond depressed and desperately needed help. When I finally made the decision to confront my reality, forgive myself, acknowledge myself, dream bigger, and dive deeper, everything began to change for the better.

Making the decision to consciously dive deeply into your life is like an outer-body experience that you crave, desire, and want to have again and again. I've learned that if you take the time to be truly present with yourself, to honestly acknowledge your actions, and keenly embrace your choices, this is where you can get to your ground zero with no baggage. This is where you need to be to start your journey upward.

The goal is to climb to the top of your mountain. The question you need to ask yourself first is, "Why haven't I climbed to the top of my mountain already?"

Next, you need to make a solid plan on how you will get to the top of your mountain. Don't skate around the edges. Don't let the world's influence direct your course of actions. And don't tiptoe cautiously around while creating your plan to get to the top of your mountain.

Go all in. Take the plunge. Jump energetically, and dive deeply into the person you want to be. Take the plunge now. Take the plunge courageously. And take the plunge fearlessly.

The series of unforeseen tragic events that happened during that time actually happened for me, and not to me. Being admitted to behavioral health facilities due to my severe depression was truly the saddest, loneliest, and most difficult time of my life.

There I was, existing as the man I thought to be: Mr. Positivity, Mr. Happy, and Mr. Successful. In reality, I was Mr. Negativity, Mr. Sad, and Mr. Very Unsuccessful. I was in a behavioral health treatment facility surrounded by negativity, sadness, and lost spirits. The icing on the cake was that I was the one who placed myself there.

It makes me happy that I live an overall healthy lifestyle. As a kid growing up with severe asthma, I always had to take lots of prescribed medications. As an adult, I am proud to be anti-medication. I won't take a simple Ibuprofen unless something is very wrong. The reality of being released from the behavioral health facility to my mother, who had to sign for me to pick me up, came with a gut-wrenching prescription for depression medication, and this shook my soul to the core.

A few days later, I changed my living situation and moved to where my mother was, in another state. After a few weeks of taking the depression medication, I felt constantly like I was living in the clouds, and I began to want the old Karma back.

I desperately wanted to be the Karma that I once knew, cherished, and adored—the Karma that was all about happiness, nutrition, health, and living life to the fullest every day. I wanted that Karma back so badly and couldn't believe I had to take depression pills every day just to get through each day.

It was like an internal battle with myself, similar to a nightmare that you can't seem to wake up from. I told myself that I could have the old Karma back without those pills and that I could reinvent myself into an even better version of myself than I was before.

Although my mother wasn't sure if it was the smartest move to suddenly stop taking the depression medication, and the doctor didn't advise it either, I made the commitment and the choice to do so. After stopping the medication, I still felt some sadness day to day, but because I was on an intentional mission to improve my mind, body, and spirit, I was not sad and depressed anymore. I was ready to climb to the top of my mountain and out of the deep, dark hole that I had self-chosen to live in.

I spent my time outside of my part-time job stocking shelves at Walmart in a new city and state, absorbing as many motivational videos on YouTube as I could handle. David Goggins, Tony Robbins, Oprah Winfrey, Tyler Perry, Jay Shetty, Lewis Howes, Eric Thomas, and Les Brown soon became the people in my life that I looked forward to being educated and motivated by every day. I would watch their videos all day long.

When I woke up in the mornings, I would immediately begin to watch their videos. On my lunch break at work, I was ecstatic to watch their uplifting videos. When I had free time at night in bed or while cooking elaborate gourmet meals in the kitchen, I had their inspiring videos playing. They truly assisted in getting me out of a constant depressed mindset and into an inspired, engaged, and encouraged mindset that was fueled and ready to take on all the great things life has to offer.

A sincere, heartfelt thank you goes out to all of the motivational speakers I mentioned. It is because of my mother, those motivational speakers, and a few people in my personal circle of family and friends that I was able to conquer severe depression and self-develop into the best version of myself that I have ever been.

Although all of those motivational speakers are incredible, and I recommend them all if you want to grow your mental health, develop strong mindfulness, and nurture your soul, there is one speaker that resonates with me and whom I gravitate toward above all the rest. Now, more than three years into my personal journey to be the best I can be in life, I still listen to, view, and follow the enlightening content from my favorite motivational teacher, Ed Mylett.

Ed Mylett has an iconic spirit that exudes passion, courage, strength, understanding, resilience, and compassion on a level like no other. On my daily course to watch a variety of motivational speakers, I find myself always seeking to watch, listen, and be inspired by Ed Mylett's personal development videos. A man that I have never met before has had such a profound impact on my life and personal growth during a time when I thought life was ending. Thank you, Ed Mylett, for being open, honest, and fueled with intent to help me and others learn how to "Be the one" and "Max out our lives." You're one of the great ones, and I am eternally grateful.

In addition to being obsessed with motivational videos because they are so fulfilling for me, I also began to meditate. As a man who prays several times per day, I find that meditating is my source to approach each day from a place of gratitude, and a place to truly connect with all of the many blessings I have, like breathing, a heartbeat, a mind, a spirit, and all of the other abundant things that surround and encompass me.

I did have some required therapy with a counselor, but I found so much growth, comfort, and gained knowledge from the sessions that, today, some years later, I continue to voluntarily work one-on-one with my therapist once a week. I've gained invaluable skills like deep breathing techniques to ignite my body into a relaxation mode that calms anger and frustration. I've been able to face and deal with events in my life that I had allowed to sustain compressed hurt, misery, anger, bitterness, and sadness—things I didn't even realize I was harboring—that ultimately were blocking my pathways to joy and fulfillment.

Thanks to my incredible therapist, Sage, I'm now able to let it "RAIN" when I'm overwhelmed with emotion. I can now:

- **R**ecognize that I am feeling a certain way.

- **A**llow the feelings to surface.

- **I**nvestigate why I am having the feelings or emotions.

- **N**urture myself by supporting myself with positivity and confidence, and find a solution to end the feelings or emotions.

When I took the time to dive deeply, I learned these and so many other skill sets in therapy that help me achieve and soar in my daily life. I'm always excited for this personal development time with my therapist. If you've never worked with a therapist, or haven't been open and honest about who you are and the life you're living, I highly encourage you to take a leap of faith and work with a great therapist that will guide you to dive deeply.

From my personal experiences, if you are willing to take the time to identify and understand what makes up the person you are, you will be able to live a more fulfilling, happy, purpose-driven, and exciting life. Dive deeply.

Habit 5:

Dive Deeply

Steps to Dive Deeply

Ask yourself a few questions, and then answer them:

How do you maneuver through life? ———

_____

_____

_____

Why do you act toward others, and react to people, the way that you do from day to day?

_____

_____

_____

Who are you spending your precious time with, and why? _____

_____

_____

_____

What activities are you allowing yourself to be involved in, and are they aligned with your morals and values? _____

_____

_____

_____

_____

_____

What makes you happy, and why? ———————

_____

_____

What is holding you back from stepping into your full potential, dreams, goals, aspirations, and passions? _____

_____

_____

_____

Do you care enough about yourself? ———

_____

_____

_____

These are some of the tough questions that helped me dive deeply into becoming the best version of myself. I strongly encourage you to spend time alone, be undistracted, and write down your honest answers to these 7 questions. It literally could be life-changing for you.

After answering these 7 questions, it is likely that you will notice at least one thing about yourself that is unsettling to you and motivates you to take a deeper look at that aspect of yourself. When you find what is unsettling, don't run away from it. Ask yourself why it's unsettling. Ask yourself what thoughts, behaviors, or beliefs are supporting that unsettling thought. Find a way to create a solution to make that unsettling thought a triumphant victory for yourself that will positively serve you.

Repeat these steps while comfortably self-exposing your reality. This is how you maximize the strengths and skill sets of diving deeply into your life. License your legacy.

Chapter 6:

MAKE THINGS HAPPEN FOR YOU AND GET RID OF THINGS HAPPENING TO YOU

Going to work every day as a Managing Partner with Texas Roadhouse wasn't like going to a job, per se. Yes, of course, I had many responsibilities and obligations, like checklists, meetings, conference calls, interviews, inventory, equipment checks, and so on. However, uniquely throughout my day, I often had the opportunity to lead the team in daily games that encouraged team development. I also participated in the line dancing our team showcased every hour in the middle of the dining room and often interacted with community organizations hosting fun-filled fundraisers and live events at my restaurant.

Almost every day was exciting for me, and I was truly living a dream lifestyle. I had reached the six-figure income level I had been after for nearly twenty years. I lived in a large house in one of the most prestigious neighborhoods in Orlando. The house was nestled among palm trees and sat alongside a beautiful lake. One of my greatest joys was swimming at midnight after work in the large, seven-foot-deep, in-ground pool in my backyard, which was enclosed by a private screened-in gazebo.

At this time, I had worked for Texas Roadhouse for 12 years and accumulated four weeks of paid vacation annually. Additionally, each year, the Managing Partner's Conference was held in a different city across America. This event was an additional week of luxury vacation for every Managing Partner and one invited guest, all paid for by the company.

The Managing Partner's Conference in San Diego offered red-carpet treatment all week, with events, poolside parties, celebrity guest speakers, and exclusive private concerts for all attendees. Memorable performances included Steven Tyler, Florida Georgia Line, and the one-and-only Snoop Dogg. Snoop Dogg was the headliner on the final evening of the conference, and to this day, I remain in awe that I attended such an incredible private concert, all thanks to Texas Roadhouse. Snoop Dogg put on an unforgettable show, filled with dancers, passion, talent, radiating energy, and, of course, his iconic rap flow that had the crowd dancing and rapping along with the D-O-Double-G.

Each year, my market managing partner also took all the managing partners in our market to a city of our choosing in the USA for pure fun and team leadership bonding. This was another week of vacation paid for by the company. Combined, I enjoyed about five weeks of paid vacations, excursions, and trips each year. These weeks provided tremendous joy, fulfillment, adventure, relaxation, and rejuvenation.

Outside of my restaurant career, I was also an independent television producer of my TV series *American Dance Legend*. I was steadily booking opportunities provided by my talent agent and finally gaining national broadcast credits and attention as an entertainer on television. I booked a national television commercial as a featured dancer for Gain Flings, which aired on Lifetime Television during *Devious Maids*. Around the same time, I was hired as a runway model for well-known companies, including Adidas, Reebok, and the PGA Tour.

It felt like the stars were aligned as more lifelong goals continued to materialize. A random audition from my talent agent sought a male who could sing, dance, and act—and I struck gold. I was booked for a starring role in a national Credit Karma television commercial as a singer, dancer, and actor. The commercial aired daily on national networks such as Lifetime, Spike, and MTV.

My phone began ringing constantly with calls from friends and family across the country congratulating me and letting me know they had seen me on TV. I was living the life I had always dreamed of, the life I had tirelessly worked to achieve. It was luxurious, plush, and, most importantly, deeply satisfying to have reached many of my dream goals.

At the time, I was in a seven-year relationship, but it began to crumble. I came to the harsh realization that friends were more important than the relationship, and that I was being taken advantage of financially and emotionally. It was crushing my happiness, breaking my heart, and dragging me down.

After seeing my sadness and distress, my closest friends and family encouraged me to move forward alone. I had given the relationship everything I had, including suggesting couples counseling, which was harshly rejected.

Admittedly, I had my own flaws to address, such as better understanding through empathy rather than sympathy and fostering open, reciprocal communication. However, as frustration and anger consumed me, I faced the harsh reality that I was being lied to repeatedly and left to fend for myself during difficult times. I couldn't handle the arguments and sadness anymore. These were red flags for me and didn't align with my values for a healthy relationship.

After significant soul-searching and self-reflection, I realized I deserved a reciprocal relationship grounded in the morals and virtues that mattered to me. I made the gut-wrenching choice to end the seven-year relationship.

Although it was heartbreaking to leave the beautiful house I lived in and take a leap of faith to move forward alone, I downsized and moved into a two-bedroom luxury apartment in a resort-style community. I was now alone in most ways and no longer had the company of the two dogs I loved so much.

The pain was often internally excruciating. Adjusting to apartment living— with neighbors above and adjacent to me—took months. I continued my rituals of spending time at the pool and barbecuing poolside, but now I shared these amenities with other tenants, lacking the privacy and comfort of my former home.

With more time alone in my apartment, I reflected deeply on my past relationship and on the broadcast of Season 3 of my television series, which had taken years to produce. Everything seemed to fall apart just after recording Season 3 and weeks before broadcasting.

I had been shopping my television series to major production companies for a national broadcast deal. Talpa, a company behind shows like *American Idol*, vetted my show but ultimately rejected it. Through a connection with my co-producer, another major production company that produced reality shows for networks like MTV considered my series. After several weeks, they too rejected it, though they acknowledged the qualities of my show and my work as an executive producer. They invited me to submit future television concepts for consideration.

I was exhausted and saddened by the workload of trying to save my series from failure. The excitement of national broadcast opportunities seemed to devolve into a cycle of constant rejection.

Producing *American Dance Legend* had been a joyous journey. I had spent years networking and building the show from nothing. To produce Season 3, I stepped down from my restaurant career and moved to Florida, far from my hometown in Virginia, to work with a production company that ultimately avoided me, leaving me to fend for myself.

Broadcasting financial troubles arose while signing contracts for multiple affiliate networks on FOX. These setbacks caused cancellations, resulting in a loss of thousands of dollars and production time for everyone involved. I felt like a failure and a disappointment to those who believed in me, which led to a deep depression.

A glimpse of hope arrived when a reputable reality television production company began considering my series. After weeks of waiting, I received an email that changed everything. I had braced myself for another rejection but instead found an acceptance offer for a partnership deal. Season 4 of my series was offered a six-figure deal with national broadcasting opportunities. With this golden acceptance, the success of the series finally seemed unstoppable.

I shared the news of the offer with my closest friends, relatives, and associates. The six-figure offer came with a hefty condition: the production company would co-own fifty percent of the series. Before accepting the offer, I shared the details with my cousin, Tichina Arnold, a television actress, and my co-producer, Pamela Bolling, an entertainment producer. Both are extremely experienced and successful in their fields, so I valued and requested their feedback.

They both warned me that the production company was being greedy by demanding fifty percent ownership of the series. They advised me to negotiate a lower percentage, and I followed their advice. However, the production company did not provide a counteroffer or agree to reduce their ownership stake. After sharing the outcome of the negotiation with my two trusted advisors, I was reminded that I had created, grown, and broadcast this series for three seasons independently through my production company. They pointed out that the offer exuded extreme greed and a lack of true partnership, which strengthened their recommendation to decline the deal.

This was my first national broadcast opportunity and by far the largest financial offer I had ever received. At this point, I had worked tirelessly for nearly five years to grow the series to its upcoming fourth season, pouring in my blood, sweat, and tears.

My heart and pride urged me to accept what seemed like an amazing offer, but my common sense and business principles told me otherwise. I faced extreme internal turmoil and conflict about the right decision. Ultimately, I braved the decision to decline the offer, rejecting the partnership due to the company's refusal to negotiate.

I tried to see this missed opportunity as a stepping stone to attract other production companies willing to offer a better partnership. Despite my optimism, I ran out of internal fuel to continue as an independent executive producer. The series, which I had nurtured for years, came to a halt, adding to my personal collection of downfalls.

Outwardly, I portrayed an upbeat, smiling, and persevering persona to my family, friends, and coworkers. Inwardly, I was torn, tattered, and deeply depressed.

I stayed focused by advancing in my restaurant career and was soon promoted to managing partner. That first year in this role was the highlight of my life, a truly life-changing opportunity. However, during this time, my relationship fell apart, and I moved out of my house to live alone. The challenges of managing the restaurant as an owner became overwhelming, even as I gave everything I had to persevere and provide solutions.

Although I tried to maintain my usual positive and courageous demeanor, those closest to me saw the deep depression consuming me. Recognizing this, I made the difficult decision to step down from my restaurant leadership role after nearly 14 years with the company. My family and friends expressed deep concern for my well-being, and I realized that the long hours I spent at the restaurant were a major contributor to my depression.

Initially, I took time off to enjoy life. I went on a cruise to the Caribbean, treated myself to an extended trip to Las Vegas, and surprised my mom with a luxurious Cirque du Soleil show and a penthouse suite. After a few months of relaxing and rejuvenating, however, my funds began to dwindle.

I embarked on a new journey to become a motivational speaker and began working on my first tour. While this new chapter was exciting, it didn't pay the bills. Despite my efforts, my plans didn't unfold as expected, and financial struggles worsened.

I applied for part-time work outside the restaurant industry but faced rejection after rejection. Employers often deemed me "overqualified" for entry-level positions due to my business ownership background. Meanwhile, a $10,000 check I was relying on to make ends meet never arrived.

Ultimately, I was evicted from my two-bedroom luxury apartment and found myself living a homeless lifestyle, moving between hotels and sleeping in my car when I couldn't afford a room.

Eventually, I secured part-time work through a staffing agency, rotating between positions as a dining room assistant at the Marriott and a line cook at the Ritz-Carlton. Despite my reluctance to return to the restaurant industry, working with top chefs at the Ritz-Carlton became a rewarding experience. I refined my culinary skills and mastered complex recipes under the guidance of highly skilled chefs.

While this opportunity gave me a temporary sense of stability, other aspects of my life continued to spiral downward. I temporarily stayed in a guesthouse provided by friends, which had been converted from a garage. Their kindness and support were invaluable, but the arrangement ended after a few months.

At my mom's suggestion, I humbled myself and rented a room in a friend's spacious home. Although it was difficult to ask for help, it was one of the best decisions I made during that time.

However, on the second day of moving my belongings to my new home, my car was repossessed. This created daily obstacles as I navigated transportation using costly ride shares, public buses, and a bicycle.

These struggles, combined with my worsening depression, led to me losing my job at the Ritz-Carlton and other subsequent positions. I cycled through various jobs, from waiting tables to selling furniture, but nothing stuck.

The final blow came when my roommate asked me to move out due to late rent payments. For the second time in less than two years, I found myself completely homeless. Without a car, funds, or support network nearby, I faced the harsh reality of living on the streets.

Out of guilt, shame, and pride, I distanced myself from family and friends who cared deeply for me. I didn't want those who thought highly of me to see me in such a broken state.

Every morning, I would ride my bicycle to my storage unit, located in a large, warehouse-style storage complex. I would fill my book bag with two days' worth of survival items, including my bulky, outdated laptop and brick-sized charger. I would stop at places with public Wi-Fi, often Panera Bread and the library, to check my emails and search for nearby job opportunities. The heavy weight of carrying so many items in my book bag on my back while riding my bicycle—day and night—created severe pain daily in my shoulders and lower back. I remember being in so much pain every day, but at the time, it didn't seem like I had a choice; I needed those necessities with me on my bicycle.

I would find slightly secluded places outside to sleep for the night—spots that weren't too far out of public sight, just in case someone tried to mess with me while I was sleeping. Bus stop waiting stations, benches at parks, and benches alongside lakes were my usual go-to spots, often just sitting up.

Every now and then, a nearby friend and their roommate would let me sleep on their couch in their home. However, I would be crowding their tiny one-bedroom home, taking up their living room space, and they both lived very busy lifestyles, so I didn't stay there much.

One early morning, I was gathering the two bags I had with me from my friend's home, where I had slept on the couch the previous night. In my usual daily routine, I had my book bag on my back, placed another travel bag on the middle rail of my bicycle, and was headed toward my storage unit, about a twenty-five-minute ride away.

While riding on the sidewalk, I came to a stop at the intersection of a driveway at a medical facility, where an SUV was pulling out. The SUV came to a stop about the same time I did. After waiting for what felt like forever, I continued riding my bicycle down the sidewalk. As I reached the front end of the SUV, the driver began to accelerate.

I didn't have time to pick up enough speed to avoid being hit. The SUV struck me, sending me, my bicycle, and my belongings crashing to the concrete. I had to pull my legs from underneath the front end of the SUV to free myself. The vehicle began to back up, and I stood up, very disoriented.

As I made eye contact with the male driver, I could sense his frustration. He shook his head and rolled his eyes at me, like I was the one who had done something wrong. He didn't seem to care much that he had just hit me. He barely spoke to me, and once he saw I wasn't bleeding or visibly broken, he sped off.

A nearby woman who had witnessed the accident walked up to me and asked if I was okay. She voluntarily exchanged information with me, offering to be a witness. I guess the driver must have seen her talking to me as he sped off because, moments later, he circled around the facility and pulled back into the parking lot where I was standing.

I'm not the type to make a big, unnecessary scene over something that can be handled calmly and civilly, so I didn't call an ambulance or the police. My ankle was hurting, and I noticed a red bruise that I hadn't seen at first, but overall, I didn't feel any major damage. I took it as grace from God and His angels watching over me once again.

This time, when the driver returned, he suddenly seemed more caring and concerned—probably because he saw there was a witness. He gave me his personal information, and with that, I gathered my two bags, got back on my bicycle, and pedaled off toward my storage unit once again.

As I rode away from the incident, I remember suddenly entering a severe state of shock. Anxiety and fear crashed over me, like the whole world had just hit me.

I cautiously and bravely kept pedaling down the sidewalk toward my storage unit, tears streaming down my face. I wanted to just lay down, rest, and process the fact that I had just been struck by a vehicle—but I had nowhere to go. No home to retreat to. I wanted to escape from the place that had become filled with nightmares, tribulations, and misery, but no matter how hard I tried, I couldn't seem to break free from any of it.

Here I was, at the lowest point of my life. I had lost everything—my relationships, my house, my luxury resort apartment, the room I was renting, my vehicle, and my almost fourteen-year career.

After being hit while riding my bicycle, feeling like there was nothing left in the world to live for, I found myself contemplating and planning suicide more than once. When friends and family found out about these thoughts, they urged me to check myself into a hospital.

I had severe anxiety and fear about stepping into any hospital. The thought alone brought me back to holding my dad's hand as he passed away in a hospital several years earlier. My mother, who was living several states away at the time, kept pushing me to check myself in.

Lost, with nowhere else to run—nowhere else but further down into the ground—I had a harsh realization. If I was ever going to rebound, succeed, and win, I had to take responsibility for my shortcomings. After a few more days of sleeping on benches, having no money for food, and no real plan to change my homeless situation—except to remove myself from the world—I finally walked into a hospital. That moment marked the start of a new chapter in my life, which, surprisingly, has turned into the best chapters of my life.

The medical staff grew concerned when I told them, in detail, about my thoughts and plans to end my life. Because I had been so open with them, they told me they were going to keep me and transfer me to a behavioral health facility. Almost immediately, I was sent to a nearby facility, where I unknowingly began the greatest comeback of my entire life.

I spent several weeks at the behavioral health facility, surrounded by men and women struggling with similar battles. Every day, I faced the man in the mirror—the same man I had once seen as successful. A restaurant owner earning six figures a year, a television producer, the star of a national TV commercial. But now, that same man sat under the watchful eyes of nurses and counselors, his every move monitored like a security threat.

Most of the people around me were trapped in their own storms—depressed, angry, overwhelmed. Some broke out in temper tantrums, others fought, many were heavily medicated. The atmosphere felt cold and heavy, a dark cloud pressing down on me daily.

Cut off from family, friends, and the outside world, I struggled to process my reality. It was painful to witness so much suffering, to feel the weight of my own mistakes. But at some point, I had to face the truth: No one else had put me here. No one else was responsible for my choices but me.

It was time to stop being a victim of my own mind. It was time to be resilient. To close this chapter—not with regret, but with resolve. It was time to move forward, to forgive myself, and to step into a new chapter of healing, prosperity, and growth.

Through counseling and months of self-imposed isolation from life's distractions and detriments, I finally took responsibility for my downfalls—something I had avoided for years as I spiraled downward.

For the first time in a long time, I felt like I was back on my own side. I stopped punishing myself for stepping out of my seven-year relationship, for walking away from my successful thirteen-year restaurant career, and—most importantly—for giving up on myself.

I didn't have a clear roadmap for what came next. I just knew I wasn't going backward. The behavioral health facility had reached out to several long-term treatment programs, places that would house me for three to six months and help me rebuild my foundation—one day at a time.

I was placed on a waiting list, released back into the world still homeless, but with something I hadn't felt in a long time: hope. Hope, drive, courage, and a new determination to win.

I was more than excited to step back into the world—free to live life on my own terms. But freedom also came with uncertainty. I had no plan—or even the faintest idea—of where I would go next. I was still waiting for a call from one of the transitional living facilities where my name sat on a waiting list. The uncertainty was gut-wrenching, nerve-wracking, and filled with every fearful emotion imaginable.

THEN, A MIRACLE ARRIVED.

The day I had longed for—the day I would leave the facility and reclaim my place in the world—was finally here. After weeks of deep self-reflection and life-changing realizations, I was being released. I had another shot at life, another chance to move forward on my own terms.

It felt like a victory I wasn't sure I would ever see.

I was escorted out of the small unit where I had been staying and taken to the main entrance—the exit. My personal belongings, which had been kept from me throughout my stay, were returned. I was eager to grab them and walk out as fast as possible. But just as I reached for them, a guard stopped me.

"Someone's here to sign you out," he said.

I couldn't imagine who would possibly be there to sign me out. Most of my closest friends and family had no idea I had been in the facility, and my mom—the only one who knew—lived several states away, far from Orlando.

The guard led me down a hallway, then around a corner. And that's when I saw her.

Standing there, glowing like an angel, was my mom.

A surge of happiness, the kind I hadn't felt in so long, flooded my entire being. It filled me from the inside out, creating a force field of pure euphoria. I was overwhelmed—shocked, elated, unable to believe what I was seeing.

As always, she wore that radiant smile—the one that could light up any room.

Without thinking, I ran to her, wrapped my arms around her, and lifted her off her feet. Spinning her in circles, I held her tighter than I ever had before, as if I could somehow make up for all the lost time in a single embrace.

I thought I had experienced the highest levels of happiness and excitement at other times in my life, but this moment was unlike any other—off the charts, and it will forever remain profoundly touching and unforgettable to me.

As a grown man, my hero—my mom—had once again traveled many miles across the country to support me in this new chapter of rebuilding and to rescue me from the grip of the world's wrath and negativity that I had previously allowed to overwhelm my mentality.

I left Orlando to regroup and visit my mom for two weeks. Truth be told, she insisted that I come see her. What began as a simple two-week "visit" ended up changing my life in ways I never expected, including gaining an incredible friend and creating a new home for the next several years.

I remain deeply grateful and incredibly blessed to have my amazing, supportive, and loving mom. Thank you, Mom, for teaching me without words how to let love overcome any obstacle, challenge, or setback!

I was no longer homeless and sleeping on an outdoor bench. I had secured a stocking job with the leading global retail chain, Walmart. The leaders and associates welcomed me with support, kindness, respect, and opportunities, for which I will forever be thankful.

My new job gave me significantly more personal time each day outside of work than I was accustomed to. Now, I was working only eight hours a day, compared to my previous career, where I was putting in a minimum of 10 hours. I used the extra hours each day to reconnect with myself.

During this time, I created a daily routine that propelled me to have an exciting, engaging, and successful day, every day. The secret to this simplicity and power lies in identifying what you're grateful for and pairing it with 3 "M's": Meditation, Motivation, and Music.

My focus was intentional—using my time outside of work to reconnect with my mom on a deeper level and be of service to others. My goal is to inspire, uplift, entertain, and empower generations.

When I opened my protective boundaries, I discovered just how much fun I was having. I went on city tours, excursions, and mountaintop vacations with my mom, new family, and friends. On the rebound, as I embraced living life daily with passion, purpose, and perseverance, I became filled with a joyful sense of fulfillment through producing motivational content, branding clothing and accessories, and writing this book.

I took responsibility for my shortcomings, failures, and weaknesses. When I did, my life turned around, and everything became so much better. I stopped beating myself up internally and stopped blaming the world for my personal issues. I took massive daily action to become the best version of myself that I could possibly be.

It was a consistent journey of a two-year decline, where I felt as if I had fallen into a deep pit, flat on my face. Now, several years later, I proudly, courageously, and with the intent to serve others, boldly stand as the best version of myself I have ever known.

Every day, I am filled with joy, happiness, and abundance, and it feels amazing. I am no longer lying flat in a pit, sad, depressed, alone, and lost. I am climbing the mountainside of life with victory, purpose, and treasure in my backpack. I'm getting closer and closer to my goal of standing at the top of my life's mountain, at the highest peak, where I envision the most beautiful sights I have ever seen.

I will forever be grateful to my angelic mother and those closest to me who helped me through the darkest time of my life when I thought it was all over. The truth is, the best part of life has just begun.

Take responsibility for your shortcomings. I strongly encourage you not to blame others for your circumstances or your position in life. Be brave, be bold, and look deeply into the person you see in the mirror.

The world will always throw setbacks, roadblocks, and dead-ends your way. It's up to you—and only you—to turn these challenges into opportunities. It's up to you to use your anger, sadness, and frustrations as fuel to ignite a fire of triumph while overcoming your shortcomings.

66

"Be the one who, at the end of your journey, can look back and be proud of achieving your greatest potential, your destiny, and your true greatness."

The easy route is to blame your upbringing, your parents, your friends, your teachers, and even your politicians. It's difficult to stop blaming others because it feels like an easy escape on the surface. But it's even more difficult to look intently at your flaws, the actions that have created obstacles, and the collection of baggage you've accumulated on your life journey.

Anyone can take the easy route of blaming others for their shortcomings. Don't be that person. Be the one who makes the change in your life that helps you reach the goals you've set for yourself. Be the one who will make a positive difference for your family, your friends, your community, and your life. Be the one who steps up to the plate and takes one big swing that hits a home run. Be the one you are proud of. Be the one you aspire to be. Be the one who, at the end of your journey, can look back and be proud of achieving your greatest potential, your destiny, and your true greatness.

While taking responsibility for your shortcomings, focus on the beautiful spirit that lives inside you. Identify, adjust, and take massive action on the next chapter—the best chapter of your life. Take responsibility for your shortcomings.

Habit 6:
Take Responsibility of Shortcomings
Steps to Take Responsibility for Shortcomings

Take Ownership

Identify your current levels in several areas of your life. Rate yourself on a scale from 1 to 10, with 1 being the lowest and 10 being the highest, based on how you feel about your current status in that area:

	1	2	3	4	5	6	7	8	9	10
Relationships	☆	☆	☆	☆	☆	☆	☆	☆	☆	☆
Education	☆	☆	☆	☆	☆	☆	☆	☆	☆	☆
Health	☆	☆	☆	☆	☆	☆	☆	☆	☆	☆
Finances	☆	☆	☆	☆	☆	☆	☆	☆	☆	☆
Love	☆	☆	☆	☆	☆	☆	☆	☆	☆	☆

What steps do you need to take in each area listed above to rate yourself a 10 in each area?

I need to work on _____

_____

_____

_____

_____ to rate myself a 10
Relationships.

I need to work on _____

_____

_____

_____ to rate myself a 10
Education.

I need to work on _____

_____

_____

_____ to rate myself a 10
Health.

I need to work on _____

_____

_____

_____

_____ to rate myself a 10
Finances.

I need to work on _____

_____

_____

_____ to rate myself a
10 **Love**.

Chapter 7:

BUILD YOUR BRIDGE TO GREATNESS WITH YOUR HEART

A s a young spirit, I was very conscious of other people's perceptions, visions, and thoughts about me as I navigated through the world. When people would meet me, there was always a strong reaction to my name. When introduced by my mother, a friend, or a family member, and they learned my name was Karma, there was always a sudden response. The reaction was always either positive or negative, with very few neutral reactions.

I'd often get the excited extreme of, "Oh, you must be the good karma I've been searching for!" and, just as quickly, some random stranger would start rubbing my arm as if I were a good luck charm. I'm not sure why, but older women seem particularly drawn to speak with me and grab onto my arms or hands when they find out my name is Karma.

On the other side, I would sometimes experience the complete opposite — negative energy. People would say, "Oh no, what have I done wrong?" and then either shy away from me, avoid eye contact, or act as if I were a bad omen. Being someone who is naturally calm, positive, and easygoing, these dramatic reactions always kept me on alert. I became extra cautious in my approach when meeting new people, never quite sure how they would react upon hearing my name.

One time, I had an audition through my talent agent for a television commercial. It was the usual cattle call, lined up with dozens of personalities and talents, each waiting for their turn. As part of the process, the director and producers asked everyone to state their name. They went down the line —

"I'm Sarah."

"My name is Kelly."

"I'm Bill."

When it was my turn, I smiled and said, "Hi, I'm Karma."

For some reason, the director stopped in his tracks, took a step back, and looked at me. "Your name is Karma?" he asked, intrigued. Unlike the others, I suddenly had an unexpected moment to introduce myself with more time and attention than anyone else in the casting line. That moment turned out to be one of the most profound auditions of my life.

I booked my first starring role in a national television commercial for Credit Karma, which aired on major networks like Bravo, MTV, BET, and Lifetime. The ad, titled Credit Karma TV Spot: 'You Deserve Better: The Musical,' became a pivotal moment in my career—one that reminded me how something as simple as a name can shape the course of an opportunity.

To be honest, the rest of the audition process—on-camera acting and dancing—wasn't my best, at least in my opinion. But the director was captivated by my name, Karma, and the fact that I could sing, dance, and act as the role required. That experience, where I had once worried about how others reacted to my name, ended up teaching me an important lesson.

It showed me how I could connect with someone in a positive and genuine way—simply by embracing my name and talents. More importantly, it became a life-changing opportunity.

Fast forward to my early twenties. One evening, I was out at a local performance venue that had a bar and club attached to it. One of my closest friends worked there as a bartender, so my inner circle and I often visited for concerts, social gatherings, or just to unwind after a long day.

That particular night, I was having a great time with friends when I found myself alone for a moment near the front door. Out of nowhere, a man approached me with a level of familiarity that caught me off guard. He spoke as if we had known each other forever, yet I had no recollection of ever meeting him.

As he carried on the conversation, he suddenly said, "Hey, you're that guy from that *Hey, what's up?* Fox commercial."

At the time, the Fox Network in the Hampton Roads area of Virginia had changed channel numbers and was running commercials where I played one of three lead roles in a parody of the famous Budweiser *"What's Up?"* ads.

Fortunately for me, these commercials aired non-stop on the local Fox Network. So, when I found myself in a conversation with this guy—who I initially thought was just a fan—I didn't expect things to take a turn. As I engaged with him positively, he suddenly became angry, his frustration escalating into outright rage. The situation turned dangerous fast.

I responded calmly, "Yeah, I had a great opportunity to work with some other actors on that commercial you saw."

His face twisted as he snapped back, "Oh, you're Karma. I heard about you. I saw you in that damn commercial. I hate that f***ing commercial."

His words were slurred, his breath thick with alcohol. His drunken ranting grew more hostile, and before I knew it, he was up in my face, pushing me back against the wall where I had been standing.

In that moment, I felt something switch inside me. I could feel the heat of my own anger rising because one thing I can't stand—one thing that triggers me instantly—is being touched by a stranger. And being shoved with force? That's a whole different level.

The drink in my hand spilled all over me, and I had to steady myself to keep from falling. Before I could fully process what had happened, my good friend—the bartender at the venue—vaulted over the bar from his service well across the room. In a flash, he yanked the guy away from me, shoving him back while yelling at him. By the grace of God—and the loyalty of a true friend I had known and worked with for years—I didn't have to react in self-defense. Otherwise, that moment could have turned into a much worse situation for both of us.

Moments like these have sharpened my instincts, making me highly attuned to people's emotions, perceptions, and body language from the second I meet them. If there's one thing I can confidently say about myself, it's that I can read people fast—whether they're good, bad, or anywhere in between.

From a very young age, I knew it was important to me to make others laugh, smile, feel joy, and be entertained. I felt a lifelong compulsion to be there for people, always wanting to lift them up. But in doing so, I often neglected to check in with myself—my true inner feelings and the quiet battles of my mind, heart, and spirit.

Without realizing it, I spent years chasing incredible goals and massive achievements, but with intentions that were, at times, misguided—fame, fortune, and an endless worry about how others perceived me. This pursuit left deep wounds, chipping away at my sense of self. In moments when I needed love the most, I found that I wasn't truly giving it to myself.

I wasn't getting intimate with my own thoughts, feelings, values, or weaknesses. I wasn't being honest with myself about who I truly was, based on my own desires—not on the world's expectations. I wasn't living as if I were an uncaring toddler—one who didn't worry about outside opinions. A toddler who greeted each day with excitement, adventure, and joy. A toddler who, without hesitation, faced problems as they came, until any panic, fear, or worry mysteriously faded away.

I encourage you to tap into your inner toddler—the part of you that finds joy effortlessly, that laughs freely, and that embraces life with wide-eyed wonder. Seek out the energy of those around you who make you feel alive, who lift your spirit, and who allow you to exist in a space where you feel happy, comfortable, and carefree in your daily life.

Take it a step further—understand why those people and moments bring you joy. When you do, you'll gain the strength and insight needed to shape your intentions with clarity and purpose.

Recognize the strengths within yourself—the very qualities that make you the powerful, beautiful spirit you are. You are capable of overcoming any obstacle, pushing past any barrier, and reaching heights beyond your wildest dreams. You are a one-of-a-kind soul, a human being who was given a one-in-a-trillion chance to exist in this world. Honor that. Take the time to know yourself, embrace yourself, understand yourself, and most importantly—love yourself.

Growing up through high school and into my early twenties, I had my fair share of dating relationships. More often than not, I was the one steering the relationship, the one leading the way and keeping things together. In all that time, I had only ever been rejected by one high school sweetheart—the one girl I had chased for years but who never quite sealed the deal with me the way I had hoped.

She was sweet, kind, and had a smile that could light up a room. Her talent was undeniable—she could sing, she could dance, and I was completely in awe of her. We both attended a performing arts school, and she was so gifted that she was chosen to be a background singer on Michael Jackson's *HIStory* album. I wrote her love letters, bought her gifts, and did everything I could to win her over. But no matter how hard I tried, I just wasn't the one she wanted.

Still, after years of chasing, I had one small victory—I got her to be my date for junior prom. I went all out. My parents helped me pick out a tux, and I saved up my own money to rent a limousine. When I arrived at her house, her mother saw us off, and for that one night, we rode together in style, heading off to prom in the limo.

We had an incredible time that night, dancing together and with friends, laughing, and soaking in the magic of the evening. We posed for pictures in front of the prom photographer—me in my sharp tuxedo, her in a stunning, shiny blue dress. In my mind, this was the beginning of everything I had wished for. In reality, it was just one beautiful evening, a fleeting moment that felt like a piece of heaven to me but ultimately ended with us remaining good friends.

I thought I was in love with her. Over the years, I had poured my heart out—expressing every emotion, feeling, and thought. I had made myself completely vulnerable, believing that if she truly knew how much I cared, she would see me the way I saw her. But one day, she told me I was coming on too strong. That hurt. To me, I was simply showing her I cared—checking in, making sure she knew she was important to me, willing to do anything for her. But to her, it was too much.

Even after that, we still performed together—sharing stages, touring from city to city, state to state, and even on a four-city tour of Japan. We always remained friendly and cordial, but I had to learn how to navigate that unspoken distance, to face the rejection, and to mend my heart. It took time, but eventually, I moved past the attraction. Still, it left a mark on me. It chipped away a small piece of my spirit, making me a little more guarded, a little less willing to open my heart so freely again.

For four years, I attended two high schools simultaneously—my academic school and my performing arts school, where I had a scholarship. At Great Bridge High School in Chesapeake, Virginia, I became close with another student, and over time, we formed a bond like brothers.

Our friendship extended beyond the classroom. We supported each other in everything—me cheering him on at his football games, him showing up for my performances. We participated in school rallies together, tackled honor student classes side by side, and shared countless moments of camaraderie.

Our families became just as close. My mom would often invite him over for dinner or sleepovers, and his mom did the same for me. I became part of his family, welcomed by his mother, father, and sister. He became part of mine, embraced by my mom and dad. It wasn't just a friendship—it was a brotherhood, one that shaped some of the best years of my life.

We were part of a larger group of students who fell into the "popular" crowd—athletes, honor roll students, and school leaders. Many of us were recognized with senior superlatives, like "High School King and Queen." I was honored to be voted both "Most Talented Male" and "Most Likely to Succeed," but the school required me to choose just one for our senior yearbook. I ultimately decided on "Most Talented Male," wanting to be remembered for the gifts and abilities my peers had come to know me for.

Great Bridge High School had a fair mix of diversity, but there weren't many Black students in honors classes. Having my best friend there with me in those courses made all the difference. We pushed each other to succeed, tackling challenging assignments together—long nights spent poring over history and English chapters, helping each other stay on top of our studies. In an environment where we sometimes felt like the minority, our bond gave us a sense of strength and belonging.

It gave both of us a sense of pride and validation—two young Black men pushing forward and proving ourselves. And after four years of hard work, we both crossed the finish line, graduating with honors at the top of our high school class.

Right after graduation, I left Virginia and moved to California for college. When winter break rolled around, I came back home, and that's when I reconnected with him—my high school brother, my best friend. He was also home from his college, and it felt like no time had passed.

We hit the town, catching up on everything—our first few months away, new experiences, the highs, the lows. It was like stepping right back into our rhythm, easy and familiar. That night was nothing short of amazing—pure fun, just like the old days.

As we strolled through a courtyard, swapping stories about college life— his at a well-known Black college, mine at a well-regarded arts school—I felt this pull to open up about something that had really shaken me. It wasn't just any story; it was something that had left a mark on me.

At that moment, I made a choice—I decided to open up about something I had buried deep inside. After years of brotherly friendship, I trusted him in a way I didn't even trust my own parents. I believed he would listen, understand, and offer the same steady guidance and support he always had.

But instead of the response I expected, something I never saw coming unfolded. His face twisted with anger—pure, unfiltered rage. I had never seen him like that, not once in the four years I had known him. Then, out of nowhere, he started yelling, cursing, his voice cutting through the night like a blade.

His whole body tensed, muscles bulking up like he was gearing up for a fight. Before I could process what was happening, he stepped in close— too close. In one swift move, he grabbed my pants with one hand, my top with the other, lifted me off the ground, and slammed me onto the cement.

Pain exploded through my back as I lay there, stunned, alone, struggling to breathe.

I reached for my phone and called my dad. His voice was urgent but calm. "Stay where you are," he said. "I'm coming." There was no one around to help, no one to witness what had just happened.

Minutes later, he pulled up, took one look at me, and rushed me to the hospital. The pain in my back was unbearable, every movement sending shockwaves through my body. I needed X-rays. I needed answers. But more than anything, I needed to understand how my best friend had just done this to me.

I was in numbing pain—inside and out. The physical agony was one thing, but the deeper wound was knowing that my best friend, the brother I never had, had done this to me. He had attacked me, violently, without hesitation. No remorse. No compassion. And after leaving me injured and helpless, he simply walked away.

By God's protecting grace, my injuries, though painful, were not life-threatening. No broken bones. No internal bleeding. But the emotional scars? Those ran deeper than any X-ray could reveal.

My parents—fiercely protective as always—were furious. They wanted justice. They reminded me that responding with violence would only add another wrong to the situation. Instead, they urged me to take the right course of action: filing a lawsuit against him.

I wrestled with that decision, torn between loyalty and self-respect. A part of me didn't want to believe this had happened. Another part of me wanted to move on, to pretend it never did. But ignoring it wouldn't erase the betrayal. And so, after much torment, I made the painful choice to take civil court legal action.

Still, deep down, I wished there was another way. Because no matter what had happened, pressing charges against the person I had once called my best friend felt like the last thing I ever wanted to do.

I came to a harsh realization—our brotherhood didn't matter in that moment. No amount of history, trust, or friendship had stopped him from physically assaulting me. And no matter how much it hurt to accept, it was only right that he be held accountable for his actions, including repaying the medical costs my parents had to cover out of their own pockets because of his violent aggression.

That experience changed me. It made me guarded. I found myself shutting down, unwilling to let anyone get too close. I had once opened my heart to a friend I loved like family, and in return, I had been betrayed. So I built walls—tall, thick, and unbreakable. It took years to even begin chipping away at them, years to untangle the pain of that moment from the way I moved through life.

As a young man, I let that and other bad experiences dictate how I approached friendships and relationships. I feared deception, false-heartedness, selfishness, envy, and negativity. I didn't trust people's intentions, always questioning whether they were genuine or just another version of the betrayal I had already endured. The vulnerability I had shown that day became a wound that never fully healed, shaping the way I engaged with friends, family, and even professional relationships.

Luckily, in my pursuit of self-improvement—mentally, physically, and spiritually—I eventually realized the walls I had built were not protecting me; they were isolating me. For years, I had unknowingly trapped myself behind these barriers, preventing myself from openly and honestly loving others. But with time, growth, and deep reflection, I became committed to breaking free. It took tremendous effort, dedication, and a sincere desire to embrace love—not just as a concept, but as an action. I wanted to love others as they were, without fear or hesitation.

I had been in past relationships where abuse, selfishness, neglect, and deceit overshadowed love. Each betrayal, each moment of pain, reinforced the belief that letting people in would only lead to suffering. I allowed those experiences to push me into deep, consuming depression—one that nearly cost me everything.

But I refused to let my past define my future. I made a conscious choice to reclaim my strength, to rebuild my trust in others, and to realign myself with the purpose and path that God had intended for me. Along this journey, I identified a few key truths—lessons that became the foundation for my healing and growth.

First, I came to a profound realization—it was not the other person, but me, who had allowed myself to enter and remain in those situations. Recognizing this gave me back my power.

Second, I understood that holding onto hate, anger, or resentment would only take up space within me—space that could be filled with prosperity, hope, love, and positivity. True healing required authentic forgiveness. Not just in words, but in my heart.

Third, I realized that, despite the pain, I had to continue seeking the love in my heart for this person—not because they deserved it, but because I deserved peace. Above all mishaps and negative experiences, love had to remain my anchor. It is love that brings joy to my heart, peace to my soul, and music to my ears.

Every day, I am reminded that love is a choice. A continuous challenge. A guiding force that shapes every relationship—new or old, personal or professional. Choosing love requires commitment. It demands understanding. But the choice is always ours to make.

So I encourage you—choose love. Be non-judgmental, compassionate, forgiving, and loyal in how you love others. When you do, you'll discover a life that is fuller, more energized, and abundant in joy. A life that is truly yours to live—free, whole, and fulfilled.

It was a cold, wintry, snow-filled season in Virginia. The Performing Arts Department was buzzing with excitement, and my talented, fun, and festive co-performers were in high spirits, soaking in the joy of the Christmas season. As the Production Manager for the department's touring performance groups, I was often at the forefront of organizing and leading many of our activities.

That particular year, I must have been either a junior or a sophomore in high school. Wanting to bring an extra layer of holiday cheer, I decided to coordinate a Secret Santa gift exchange. It was a way to give those who wanted to participate an opportunity to show kindness and appreciation for one another during the season.

66

"Be non-judgmental, compassionate, forgiving, and loyal in how you love others."

Each participant randomly drew a name and was responsible for bringing a gift for that person—keeping their identity a secret until the big reveal. Since I was organizing the event, I was the only one who knew who had drawn whom. I took that responsibility seriously, making sure not to spill any secrets so the excitement and suspense would build up until the exchange.

The group of about twenty-five participants made an effort to be thoughtful, sending close friends on secret missions to gather intel about what their chosen person liked. They did so with impressive stealth and undercover skills, ensuring no one discovered their Secret Santa too soon.

Without a doubt, it was fun watching everyone scramble to find the perfect gift. For me—the keeper of the master list of Secret Santas—it was equally entertaining and, at times, a little stressful. I had to listen to everyone's wild guesses while keeping a straight face. This coordinated chaos went on for about two weeks.

Finally, the big day arrived. Everyone brought in their carefully chosen gifts, eager to reveal their surprises. Among the students participating were several from my academic high school, Great Bridge High School, who also attended the Governor's School for the Arts each afternoon. One of them—let's call her Wendy to protect her real identity—was in the Performing Arts Department with me.

Every school day, we all took the same bus from Great Bridge High School to the Governor's School for the Arts. During this time, while the Secret Santa exchange was in full swing, Wendy sat in the back of the bus near me. One day, she quietly confided that her family was going through tough times and that she couldn't afford to buy a gift for the person she had drawn.

I felt awful for Wendy—she clearly wanted to participate but couldn't. At the same time, I felt for the person she had chosen, who wouldn't be receiving a gift despite having bought one for someone else.

I wanted everyone to enjoy the exchange, so I came up with a simple solution. That evening, after school, I asked my parents to take me to the store. Since I knew who Wendy's chosen person was and had a good idea of what they might like, I picked out a thoughtful gift, wrapped it neatly with festive paper, and tied it with a bow.

The next day—Secret Santa gift exchange day—I was super excited to tell Wendy that she now had a gift to give to her chosen person. As usual, we all boarded the school bus from Great Bridge High School to the Governor's School for the Arts. I sat in my seat, eagerly waiting for Wendy to get on.

When she finally boarded and walked past my seat, I reached out, holding the gift in my hand. Smiling, I told her that I had gone to the store the night before and picked out something for her chosen person, so she didn't have to worry. Before she could protest, I reassured her that there was no need to pay me back—it was my gift to her, so she could fully take part in the exchange.

What I thought would be a magical moment turned into a complete disaster. Wendy's face scrunched with anger, her cheeks flushed red, and before I could even process what was happening, she exploded. She started yelling at me, snatched the gift out of my hand, and hurled it across the school bus floor before storming to the back.

I was devastated. My heart felt like it had been shattered on the spot. A wave of anger and hurt crashed over me. I had spent my time, energy, and money—not to mention my parents' time—to help her out during what was already a tough season for her and her family. And this was how she reacted? She didn't just reject my kindness; she threw it on the ground— literally. Not even a whisper of thanks. It blew my mind.

For years, I carried a deep, simmering resentment toward Wendy. The gift still made its way to her chosen person, but the damage had already been done. Eventually, my peers and the department found out what had happened because my usual upbeat, positive self was visibly shaken. They knew something was wrong. I was hurt, angry, and just plain sad about the whole thing.

People tried to get me to forgive Wendy, but I just couldn't let it go. For the last few years we had together in performing arts classes, shows, and even a tour to Japan, I couldn't stand the sight of her. I refused to speak to her unless it was absolutely necessary for my Production Manager duties. Otherwise, I avoided her like the plague.

Every time she had a solo on stage, I despised every note she sang—no matter how undeniably talented she was. The anger ran deep. If I was being honest, I had real hate for her. She was the only person I had ever disliked on such a serious level.

But after high school, as I navigated early adulthood, I started to understand the weight of forgiveness in a way I never had before. I realized that holding onto that kind of anger only chained me to the past. Letting go wasn't about excusing her actions—it was about freeing myself.

As I stepped into management roles in restaurant operations, I often found myself in the position of teaching others about forgiveness. In tough conversations, I had to guide people toward being the bigger person, helping them see the power in apologizing and finding resolution, even when it wasn't easy.

I always prided myself on not letting someone else's anger, issues, or negativity take up my time, thoughts, or energy. But there was one person from high school I just couldn't stand. For years, I held onto that resentment like it was a part of me.

As an adult, though, I made a choice—I forgave Wendy. Not for her, but for me. I didn't want those negative feelings taking up space inside me, space that could be filled with things that actually mattered.

Maybe Wendy was just going through something when she snatched the gift out of my hand and threw it across the bus. Maybe she was embarrassed that she couldn't afford a gift for her person and had no idea how to deal with that feeling. Or maybe she just hated the holiday season. Maybe it had nothing to do with me at all—even though, at the time, it felt like a personal attack.

So I chose to remember the good things. The ridiculous bus rides full of laughter and chaos. The partnership we built as new freshmen, both navigating our academic high school and the cutthroat world of our Performing Arts department—a place packed with talent, where bonds were formed long before we even arrived. A world we survived together.

I chose to remember the support and respect we had for each other during our first few years of high school. I chose to hold onto the memories of the incredible stages, theaters, and tours we shared—where we grew as artists together. I chose to forgive Wendy for that one outburst on the school bus. I chose to love Wendy as the co-performer and peer who, in the beginning, felt like a sister. I chose to cherish the great times we had together, to let go of the resentment, and to replace it with love.

After making the conscious decision to embrace people as they are—especially Wendy—I felt a heavy burden lift from my spirit.

"Wendy, if you're reading this book, you'll recognize yourself in these moments. I want you to know that I am deeply grateful for the incredible journeys we shared in high school and that I forgive you for the Secret Santa conflict. Please forgive me for

how cold I was in the years that followed. Most importantly, I want you to know that I love you like a sister, and I pray that life is bringing you all the joy and success you deserve.

Love always,

Your Performing Arts Brother,

-KARMA"

There is tremendous personal growth and significant achievement when you truly connect with the power of loving others. Loving people through both good times and bad is a skill that creates an energy that radiates around you. This energy, fueled by the love within you, will carry you through the hardest moments of your life and elevate you to the greatest joys of your dreams and reality. You will become a stronger lover, friend, partner, sibling, parent, neighbor, and individual.

The world is home to more than 7 billion people, each with unique personalities, and you will cross paths with many of them. They will shape your experiences, influence your choices, and play a role in your journey. Having a solid foundation in how to love others authentically—just as they are—will help you move through life's diverse personalities and relationships with greater understanding and grace.

You will not only attract others to you in a genuine and fulfilling way, but you will also build solid, meaningful, and lasting relationships. These connections—whether family, personal, or professional—will create a strong support system and strengthen your social circle, bringing you deep peace, gratitude, and happiness.

Loving myself and others has opened my heart, expanded my mind, and fulfilled my spirit. Now, go forward into your daily walk of life, loving yourself as the most precious and invaluable gift, because you are beautiful and extraordinary just as you are. You are here on this earth with purpose and meaning, destined to do incredible things with your life.

Run further into your journey, embracing love for others as they are. Cherish them for who they are becoming, and nurture their lives with the care and devotion of a parent cradling their newborn child. It's powerful, it's profound, and it's yours to embrace. Love yourself and love others.

Habit 7:
Love Yourself and Love Others
STEPS TO GUIDE YOUR LOVE

Take ownership and responsibility for where you are in any situation or relationship.

Don't allow hate, anger, sadness, or sorrow to consume your time, thoughts, or energy toward someone else.

Let love, joy, peace, and happy memories with others fill your heart, mind, and soul.

LOVE ACTIVITY

Strengthen your ability to love by practicing love-willingness the openness to embrace love fully. Answer the following questions honestly, without judgment of yourself or others:

What behaviors can you take ownership of to improve the way you love yourself? _____

_____

_____

_____

What behaviors can you take ownership of to improve the way you love others? _____

_____

_____

What thoughts are you currently holding onto that stem from hate, anger, sadness, or sorrow?

_____

_____

_____

_____

Imagine these thoughts as an anchor, chained to
the ocean floor, keeping a boat from moving
forward.

What recent experiences have filled you with love, joy, and peace?

_____

_____

_____

_____

Imagine these moments as a balloon, tied to a string, floating freely toward the sky.

Now that you've identified your behaviors, thoughts, and experiences, ask yourself:

Is your love-willingness dragging you downward like the anchor, keeping you stuck in place? _____

_____

_____

_____

Or is your love-willingness lifting you upward like the balloon, soaring high and moving you forward? _____

_____

_____

_____

Chapter 8:

CLEAR YOUR VISION AND GAIN EVERYTHING YOU WANT

My mother and I both hail from the city that never sleeps—**New York City, "The Big Apple."** Growing up in the Bronx, my mother was a spirited and beautiful young woman. She experienced countless joyous moments but also faced the many challenges that come with city life.

Just two months before her twentieth birthday, I made my grand entrance into the world—**two months premature.** This meant my mother became a teenage mom, something she still jokingly blames on me to this day. She likes to say, **"If you hadn't been in such a rush to be born, I wouldn't have been a teenage mother!"**

Looking back, I think my early arrival was simply a reflection of who I've always been—**excited, energized, and ready to take on the world.** Even in the womb, I imagine myself thinking, **"Let me out of here! It's too dark, and I've got things to do!"** But my eagerness came at a price—**being born prematurely caused significant complications for both my mother and me.**

My mother tells me that the doctors did everything they could to stop her from going into labor two months early, but their efforts were unsuccessful. She remained in labor for three exhausting days—**and she never lets me forget just how long those days were.**

To make things even more difficult, I wasn't in the ideal position for birth. Instead of being head-down, I was lying on her kidneys, making an already complicated situation even more painful for her.

When the long-awaited moment of birth finally arrived, I imagine it wasn't as magical as one might hope. **I struggled to breathe, and the doctors had to revive me several times because my lungs weren't fully developed.** It was a terrifying start to life, but against all odds, I survived.

Because of the extreme challenges surrounding my birth—and the miracle of my survival as a seven-month premature baby—**my mother saw me as her good karma. And that's how I got my name: Karma.**

As if my birth hadn't been challenging enough for my mother, she couldn't take me home right away. Instead, I spent six long months in an incubator, my tiny lungs still too underdeveloped to function on their own.

Each time the doctors prepared to release me, I would suffer another asthma attack, forcing them to keep me hospitalized. I can't begin to imagine the daily fear and helplessness my mother must have felt—watching her newborn struggle to breathe, unable to do anything but wait and hope. It must have taken incredible strength to face each day with courage.

Eventually, the day came when I was finally strong enough to leave the hospital. My mother and I could finally begin our life together beyond those hospital walls.

I don't remember those early months, but knowing how fragile my start in life was, I choose to carry gratitude with me every day. I see my life as a blessing—a second chance that I will never take for granted.

The probability of being born a human spirit in this world is one in three trillion. Knowing that—and understanding the challenges I faced as a premature baby—reminds me that my life is no accident. I am here for a reason. Overcoming those early obstacles tells me that I am destined for greatness, and that God has a mission and purpose for me.

My birth father and my mother were not the right fit for each other, so my incredible mom raised me on her own. She poured her love into me, giving me everything she could. She spoiled me with almost anything I wanted— not just with things, but with care and attention. She dressed me in designer clothing, custom-made hats, shirts, and accessories, all embroidered with my name: Karma.

One of my favorite and most memorable accessories was a gold-framed belt buckle with my name in big block lettering. I wore that belt all the time, and as a kid, it brought me tremendous joy.

Like any young, active child, I put that belt and its buckle through more wear and tear than it could handle. One day, after countless adventures, the final weld gave out, and the letters of my name tumbled from the frame, beyond repair. I remember feeling so sad about it, but, as always, my mom found a way to lift me up. She kept making blankets, sweatshirts, and other beautiful pieces—each one carrying my name, keeping that special connection alive.

My mom and I lived in Philadelphia, but we often traveled back and forth to New York City to visit my aunt and cousins. I always had the best time with my cousins, Rishod and Arkeena. Even though they were brother and sister, I claimed them as my own—I was the third man out, but in my mind, we were all siblings.

The three of us were like peas in a pod. We set up fake offices in my cousins' room, filling them with paper credit cards we carefully cut out from stacks of blank credit card applications we'd taken from stores. Our talent shows were legendary—we raided every closet in the house for costumes, turning the living room into our stage. I was always the mastermind behind convincing Arkeena to help me take apart toys, clocks, and electronics, just to see how they worked and if we could put them back together. It was usually an epic fail, much to the frustration of my aunt and uncle, who weren't too happy when we inevitably broke whatever we had taken apart.

I spent holidays and summers every year with my awesome Aunt Catrina, Uncle Lee, and my cousins. My aunt would take us on fun shopping trips along Third Avenue and ferry excursions to see the Statue of Liberty.

My uncle would bring us downtown to Manhattan, where his relatives lived, and that's where the real fun happened—block parties, basketball tournaments, and more cousins and kids than we could count, all running wild in the park. Uncle Lee was always at the grill, flipping burgers, hot dogs, and ribs, or roasting a whole pig over the fire pit. And no visit was complete without him spoiling us with Swedish Fish candy and submarine sandwiches from the corner store deli.

Inside the house, my aunt kept us well-fed with her home-cooked meals—her lasagna and sausage with broccoli were my favorites. But nothing compared to getting Chinese food from the local spot. Ask anyone in my family, and they'll tell you how much I loved and adored that Chinese food. If you've never been to New York City, let me tell you—without a doubt, it has the best Chinese food in America.

One time, after we were back home in Philadelphia, my mom introduced me to her friend Eddie. Eddie had a vibrant smile and an energy that could light up a room—warm, dynamic, and full of care. He wore black-lensed Hollywood-style glasses with gold frames, a sharp business suit with a tie, and shiny, pointed shoes. This man was put together from head to toe. And his car? A sleek, shiny Lincoln Town Car that looked straight out of a Batman movie.

Eddie was a regional manager for IBM, handling copy machines for businesses, which meant he had access to all kinds of colorful copy paper. He knew about my love for paper, creativity, and the color orange. One of the first times we met, he brought me a roll of orange-colored paper. I had never seen anything like it before—it looked just like a jumbo-sized paper towel roll but was pure orange. That roll of paper seemed endless, and I had the time of my life with it.

Eddie would take my mom and me to fancy restaurants and on fun trips around Philadelphia in his Batmobile. He showed us historical sites and even brought us to his office at IBM, inside one of the two towering Liberty buildings that dominated the city skyline. We were so high up in the sky, surrounded by gleaming glass windows, that it felt like we were floating on clouds. The view was breathtaking.

Inside his office, I was mesmerized by the rows of IBM computers and the massive copy machines—some as big as a small car. It was like stepping into the future.

One day, on one of our adventures in the Batmobile, we drove far beyond Philadelphia. Eddie and my mom took me to a beautiful, upscale, quiet town called Devon. We parked in front of a grassy hill in a small community with both short and tall houses connected to each other—what I now know were condominiums.

Two flights of stairs led down to an underground basement, where Eddie stored an eclectic collection of items—treasures tucked away beneath this towering home.

We climbed the wide cement steps, reaching the top of the grassy hill, where Eddie led us to the front door of a corner unit in the towering condominium complex. They told me this was Eddie's home.

Stepping inside, the place felt like a humongous castle. The entry-level floor had a bathroom and a closet in the hallway, right next to the spacious kitchen, which seamlessly connected to the dining room. You could enter the dining room from the hallway or directly through the kitchen. But once you stood in the dining room, the view hit you—it was mesmerizing and took your breath away.

Leaning over the banister, you took in the sight of a magnificent two-story unit, its glass doors and floor-to-ceiling windows framing an expansive suburban view. Below, a sunken living room sprawled out—enormous, almost unreal. It was packed with couches, sofas, a sleek glass centerpiece table, and a massive floor-unit family television. By far, the largest living room I had ever seen.

Two flights of stairs led down to an underground basement, where Eddie stored a collection of items—some neatly packed, others scattered like forgotten memories.

I was already thrilled beyond words. From the main floor, we climbed two flights of winding stairs to the top level. A hallway stretched in both directions—left and right. We went left first.

At the end of the hall was the master bedroom, a grand space featuring a large bedroom suite, an entertainment center, and a luxurious bathroom. Behind sleek sliding doors, a walk-in closet was tucked away like a hidden treasure.

Then we crossed the hall to another room.

This room was enormous—almost like two rooms in one. On the left, it resembled another living room, complete with a sofa bed and a cozy sitting area that framed a stunning corner-window view of the picturesque suburban town. On the right, a spacious, open area stood nearly empty, except for a small gray desk with a large typewriter resting on top.

Eddie let me sit and use his typewriter. I thought it was the most amazing thing ever. The moving arms and sliding pieces fascinated me as they stamped letters onto the paper fed into the roller pin. It felt like I had stepped into a magical playground.

Later, my mom asked if I liked Eddie's house. Of course, I answered with an enthusiastic, "Yes!"

Then came the question that would change my life.

Eddie asked, "Would you like for this to be your room and live here with me and your mom?"

It was the easiest "yes" I had ever said.

It felt like stepping into a fantasy world—a four-story magical castle in a beautiful suburban town. From that moment on, my life catapulted forward, filled with magical, inspiring, and unforgettable memories that shaped me from a five-year-old boy into the man I am today.

My mother and I moved out of Philadelphia and into the suburban town of Devon to live with Eddie. Soon after, my mom and Eddie got married. Eddie adopted me, and I took his last name, legally becoming Karma Butler.

Everyone, including my mom, called Eddie by his last name, "Butler." I thought it was so cool to share the same name—and even more incredible to have Eddie as my dad, especially since my birth father had never been in the picture.

Beyond having my own massive bedroom with an attached living area, the neighborhood was unforgettable.

Across the street stood a sprawling apartment complex with more than 20 buildings, which meant there were always kids and friends to play with. Just down the street, within walking distance, was the nationally known Devon Horse Show. When my cousins visited from New York, we would go together, watching derbies and petting the majestic Budweiser Clydesdales.

In the other direction, near my elementary school, were enormous mansions— two of which belonged to the owners of Hellmann's Mayonnaise and Campbell's Soup.

Despite early struggles with learning disabilities, I became well-known in school and the community. I was honored as Student of the Month, featured in the local newspaper as a soloist in the district chorus, and achieved high honors as a Cub Scout.

My mom, who was my den leader, brought boundless energy to our troop, making it the top-ranked group in the county. She organized fun-filled activities like roller derbies, boating trips, camping adventures, pizza parties, museum sleep-ins, and more.

As I advanced to Boy Scouts, my mom stepped down as den leader, and my dad took over. He thrived in the role, teaching us essential skills like knot-tying and guiding us in earning achievements through service to the church and community. I climbed the ranks and was on the verge of earning the coveted Eagle Scout title. However, frequent asthma attacks and a growing passion for the performing arts led me to shift my focus to a new dream.

My parents wholeheartedly supported my artistic aspirations. In a bold move, they sold their luxurious four-story condo in Devon, Pennsylvania, and relocated to Chesapeake, Virginia, so I could attend the prestigious Governor's School for the Arts in Norfolk. To ensure I could start high school on time, they first rented a house. Soon after, they built a brand-new, four-bedroom, two-story home—complete with a half-sized basketball court for my cousin Jeron and the largest in-ground pool in the neighborhood.

Balancing my demanding schedule—splitting time between Great Bridge High School for academics and the Governor's School for performing arts—was no easy feat. But through it all, my parents remained unwavering in their support. My dad often drove me to auditions, rehearsals, and tours, instilling in me a lesson that set me apart from my peers: *"To arrive early is on time, and to arrive on time is late."*

My first national acting role came through my acting teacher, Mimi, who was also a youth talent agent at a prominent agency. I landed a part on CBN, playing a rookie on a SWAT team. The shoot was exhilarating—complete with simulated gunfire and explosive effects. However, it ran late into the night, wrapping up around 3 a.m., which did *not* sit well with my mom. Furious at first, she eventually calmed down when she saw I was still excelling in school and maintaining good grades. Thankfully, she never confronted my talent agent, and I kept booking roles.

As I performed in prestigious venues like Norfolk's Chrysler Hall, my mom was always my biggest cheerleader. She packed the audience with friends, family, and neighbors, filling entire rows with her infectious enthusiasm. My performing arts director, Chip, would even set aside blocks of front-row tickets just for her—because she *always* sold out shows. At every performance, she was front and center, proudly shouting, *"That's my baby!"*

She also took on the role of my personal chauffeur, driving me to auditions near and far. One time, she drove nearly two hours from our house to Richmond, Virginia, for my audition for Paramount's Kings Dominion main stage show, *Retro Active*. She sat through the entire day, watching me— and every other performer—audition from early morning until late at night. Then, without hesitation, she drove us the two hours back home.

That audition didn't end the way I had hoped. Several of my classmates from the performing arts school landed contracts, while I was placed on the standby list—essentially, not cast. After all the time, energy, and effort my family and I had poured into that opportunity, it stung. But as I would soon learn, setbacks often set the stage for something greater.

For months, I watched as my friends, who had been cast, shared their excitement about rehearsals and moving to Richmond for their high-paying contracts. Instead of feeling defeated, I chose gratitude. I was thankful to have such talented peers who challenged me to grow. Rather than dwelling on rejection, I poured myself into my training—pushing harder in every class, absorbing every dance move and vocal technique my teachers shared. These weren't just any teachers; they were professionals from Broadway, national tours, and television, and they expected excellence.

Then, just weeks before my high school graduation, I got a phone call that changed everything. It was the stage manager of *Retro Active*. One of the dancers had dislocated their knee and was out of the show.

In that moment, all my effort and dedication paid off—I accepted my first professional dance contract with Paramount. Looking back, I truly believe my gratitude brought everything full circle.

I had been scheduled to tour and perform in Japan for the second time, but I chose Paramount instead. It was a tough decision, but one that felt right. Just before starting my contract, I graduated as valedictorian of the Governor's School for the Arts and had the honor of delivering the commencement speech. As always, my mom and dad were front and center in the theater, celebrating my four-year performing arts journey.

Their support didn't stop there. They helped me move to Richmond and even gifted me a car so I could fully commit to my summer-long contract. Performing in *Retro Active* under famed choreographer Barry Lather was an incredible experience. I worked alongside producers from television, theater, national tours, and cruise ships—connections that would shape my future. I performed three to five shows a day, earned great money for an 18-year-old, built lifelong friendships, and had the best summer of my life.

All too soon, the season came to an end. I packed up my apartment, said heartfelt goodbyes to my castmates, and returned home to Chesapeake for a few weeks—just long enough to catch my breath before my next adventure.

During my high school graduation celebrations, I was offered a scholarship to attend the California Institute of the Arts as a dance major. Once again, my heroic parents made it happen—both financially and emotionally. Just weeks after wrapping up my first stage contract, I packed my bags and moved across the country to start college in Valencia, California.

To my surprise, my mom, dad, Aunt Catrina, Uncle Lee, and cousins Arkeena and Jeron all flew with me to California to drop me off. Seeing them turn this milestone into a full-on family event meant everything to me. And just when I thought it couldn't get any better, my cousin Tichina—my angel and mentor—joined us and treated us to an unforgettable dinner in Beverly Hills.

My parents could have easily sent me off on my own, but instead, they surrounded me with love and support during this huge transition. That kind of love stays with you forever—it carved a permanent place in my heart.

As an 18-year-old living on campus on the other side of the country, I felt a deep sadness when my family flew back to Virginia. But knowing that my cousin Tichina was nearby—and that my family was just a phone call away—gave me some comfort.

Back home, my dad's health started to decline. He was in and out of the hospital, battling kidney problems and one of the worst cases of shingles the doctors had ever seen. The virus had ravaged his arm so badly that the outer layer of his skin looked burned.

He had to sleep with his arm elevated because even the slightest touch sent shockwaves of pain through his body. Watching him push through that kind of agony while staying mentally sharp was nothing short of incredible.

Though his health seemed to improve after countless hospital visits and dialysis treatments, he remained weak. But his spirit never faded—he was always laughing, always cracking jokes. Seeing him find joy despite everything gave me hope.

Then one day, his condition took a turn for the worse. After coming home from the hospital, he couldn't manage the stairs anymore, so we set up a mobile bed in the dining room. A hospice nurse started visiting daily. He smiled and laughed less, but even then, he held onto his humor and spirit.

A few weeks later, he asked to go back to the hospital. My mom and I went with him, just as we always did. In his hospital room, he cracked jokes and insisted he was "fantastic," even though we could see he was struggling.

Then the nurse came in to take him to dialysis. But instead of wheeling him out, she checked his vitals and said the words that shattered my world:

"Mr. Butler, your blood pressure is too low. We can't take you to dialysis."

The universe seemed to stop. I felt the weight of the moment settle in—dialysis was what kept him breathing and functioning.

The doctor explained that our only option was to take him to the ICU, where they would put him on ventilators and administer medication to raise his blood pressure for dialysis. Without it, he wouldn't survive.

When the doctor left, my mom stepped out of the room, fighting back tears. I stayed with my dad, and we had one of the most honest conversations of my life.

I urged him to consider the ICU option, but he met my gaze, calm and steady, and asked, **"Karma, do you really want to see your dad hooked up to a bunch of life-support machines with tubes everywhere?"**

I couldn't imagine seeing him like that. He reassured me, saying he had lived a full life and that everything would be okay. Then, with his signature humor, he added, "I'll show you how to leave this world like a king."

Even as his body grew weaker and his breathing became more labored, he kept smiling and laughing. Then he spoke the words I will never forget:

"Karma, make sure y'all get rid of that big house. Take care of your mother because she needs you, and you need her. It was such a pleasure being your dad."

At that moment, even through his laughter and warmth, it all clicked—I finally understood what he was telling me.

I let my dad rest and stepped out of the hospital room. In the hallway, I approached the doctor, needing answers I knew he wouldn't say in front of my dad. I told him that my dad had decided against the ICU—he wanted to let things take their natural course without invasive machines or drugs. Then I locked eyes with the doctor and asked the question I wasn't sure I was ready to hear the answer to.

"How long does he have to live?"

The doctor hesitated, then finally said, "Most likely, no more than a day or two."

I could tell he was being honest. I thanked him and asked him to do everything possible to keep my dad comfortable.

I couldn't convince my dad to go to the ICU to prolong his already limited time, nor could I stop what was happening or help him get better. It was the most gut-wrenching, heart-aching, and deeply sorrowful moment of my life.

But I didn't cry. I didn't break down. I knew I had to be strong for my mother.

My dad's words about "going out like a king," delivered with his signature laughter, stayed with me. Even in the face of finality, I was certain he wouldn't want me to be a broken mess.

"

"Free yourself from restrictive beliefs and step into a world of limitless possibilities."

Over the next day, my mother and I stayed by my dad's hospital bedside. He quickly began to lose consciousness. When I asked my mother what was happening, she explained that he was becoming delirious.

One last time—for the last time—I held my dad's hand, which hung from the side of the hospital bed, and squeezed it for what felt like an hour. I stepped out of the room briefly to compose myself.

When I returned, my mom looked into my eyes and said the words no son ever wants to hear: "He's gone."

I wrapped my arms around my mother, holding her with all my strength. Then, I stood tall and proud, smiling at the memory of the most amazing man I had ever known. I knew that was exactly what would make him proud—knowing that of the nearly thirty years of love, support, guidance, mentoring, and joy he had given me, his legacy would live on.

He had adopted me and been my dad—a true king.

Eddie taught me never to let others' actions dictate my happiness or control my responses. He showed me that I was not a victim of society but someone with the power to use my time and talents to contribute positively to the world.

He often told me, *"Don't let others drive your car just because they're out of control and rushing behind you, pressing on your bumper."* Instead, he urged me to stay calm and in control of my own car—the car that symbolized my life and its direction.

My mother and father, together, were a dynamic duo who gave their all: their time, love, resources, and unwavering support so I could live my best life. From my premature birth at seven months to the adult I am today, they were there—on school trips, at meetings, award ceremonies, youth groups, sports events, rehearsals, auditions, live performances, doctor visits, hospital stays, and everything in between.

They taught me to be grateful for the health, talents, and life God blessed me with. But more than that, they instilled in me the most valuable habit—one that has been instrumental in achieving my greatest successes: seeing life through a lens of gratitude.

When you look at the world through your own eyes, your perception is often shaped by old memories, limiting beliefs, and emotions like fear or anger. But you have the power to override these tendencies. By developing a conscious mindset, you can reshape how you receive information and experience the present moment.

When faced with painful memories, self-doubt, or negativity, choose to see through a lens of gratitude. Transform past struggles into lessons that fuel growth. Don't dwell on what was—focus on what *can be*. Free yourself from restrictive beliefs and step into a world of limitless possibilities. Replace anger with joy, fear with hope, and hesitation with action.

Throughout your life, there have been people who have supported, believed in, and encouraged you. Choose to appreciate both the small and significant ways they've lifted you—whether through a comforting hug, a kind word, or unwavering faith in your potential. Honor their influence by embracing gratitude as your guiding perspective.

Think of all the time, effort, and dedication you've poured into becoming the person you aspire to be. Now, step forward with confidence. **Go meet that person. Go be that person.**

By choosing to see through a lens of gratitude, you cultivate appreciation, thankfulness, and grace. These emotions generate positive energy, attracting even more positivity into your life. Gratitude isn't something that can be faked or forced—it's a powerful habit, a genuine force that highly successful individuals rely on.

When you develop this habit, you unlock a transformative power that shifts your perspective and fuels your growth. **Choose to see through a lens of gratitude.**

Habit 8:
See Through a Lens of Gratitude
Steps to Strengthen Your Gratitude Mindset

Start Your Day with Gratitude
Identify five things and five people you're grateful for. Incorporate this into your meditation, prayer, breathwork, or journaling practice.

Five things you're grateful for

- _____
- _____
- _____
- _____
- _____

Five people you're grateful for

- _____
- _____
- _____
- _____
- _____

Appreciate, Don't Envy

Observe high achievers around you. Instead of feeling resentment, analyze their strengths and behaviors. Use their success as inspiration.

_____

_____

_____

_____

_____

_____

_____

_____

_____

_____

_____

_____

Reframe Challenges as Growth

Reflect on obstacles you've overcome. When anger or frustration arises, shift your focus to the lessons learned and the positives that came from them.

_____

_____

_____

_____

_____

_____

_____

_____

_____

_____

_____

_____

_____

_____

Apologize Quickly and Authentically

Own your mistakes, whether intentional or not. A sincere apology strengthens relationships and builds integrity.

_____

_____

_____

Forgive with an Open Heart

Let go of resentment. True forgiveness whether or not an apology is given frees you from negativity and fosters peace.

_____

_____

_____

Surround Yourself with Gratitude-Filled People

Energy is contagious. Spend time with those who naturally express appreciation, and learn from their mindset. _____

_____

_____

Give Freely
Show appreciation through thoughtful gestures or acts of kindness. Give from the heart, expecting nothing in return.

Chapter 9:

SEE YOURSELF, KNOW YOURSELF, UNLOCK YOUR BEST SELF

W hile living in and around the Los Angeles area for several years, I attended college and landed appearances on several national television shows. I earned a dance scholarship at a well-known Los Angeles studio, training under celebrity choreographers like Wade Robson and Tovaris Wilson. Represented by DDO Artists Agency— one of the biggest dance agencies—I auditioned for tours, music videos, and concerts for major artists, including Britney Spears and Beyoncé.

At the height of this whirlwind, I was called back for casting in Prince's music video and award show, as well as Janet Jackson's *Velvet Rope Tour*. Dancing alongside some of the most respected and ridiculously talented professionals in the industry, I could feel myself getting closer to that upper echelon of the dance world.

I auditioned for Debbie Allen's *Fame* reality television series. Debbie and her team were looking for multi-talented, triple-threat performers who could sing, dance, and act. While I wasn't chosen as one of the 24 contestants hand-picked by Debbie Allen that season, I was in for a surprise when the show aired that summer. Friends and family from across the country called to say they had seen me performing on the show.

Getting cut from the audition stung, but I was still grateful for the experience of working with Debbie Allen—a true icon in the performance world. Her words during the audition stuck with me: *"Fame is not a destination; it's the journey you're on. Embrace it, go all out, give it your fullest energy, and enjoy the ride."* I carry her wisdom with me to this day.

I was caught up in a whirlwind of acting—auditioning for casting agents and producers, performing in theatrical productions, and juggling acting and dance classes. In between, there were fun limousine rides and celebrity events with my cousin Tichina and industry friends. It was a dream for an eager twenty-year-old, but the constant hustle took a serious toll on me—mentally, physically, and spiritually.

After years of chasing the next opportunity, pushing through exhaustion, and navigating intense competition, I reached a breaking point. My cousin and my closest friends saw what I couldn't at the time—they knew I needed to pause, breathe, and reset. One day, my cousin picked me up and insisted I go home to my parents to find my footing again. She drove me to LAX, where a ticket—sent by my parents—was waiting to fly me back to Virginia.

At the time, I didn't agree with the intervention my cousin and parents had orchestrated—especially since they hadn't included me in the planning. But my cousin, who has always had my best interests at heart, is not one to take no for an answer. Since childhood, she's been a guiding force in my life, always pushing me toward what's best for me. So, despite my resistance, I followed her lead, boarded the plane with nothing but the clothes on my back, and flew home to Virginia.

During the five-to-six-hour flight, my emotions were all over the place— excitement to see my parents, frustration at the situation, and disappointment in myself for losing my way. When they had dropped me off at California Institute of the Arts as a scholarship student, I had been set up for success. Now, I was heading back home feeling like a mess, with no clear direction.

As I sat on the flight, reflecting on everything that had led me to this moment, I started thinking about how I could make the most of my time in Virginia. Unlike Los Angeles, there were no bustling production studios or daily opportunities in the entertainment industry. But I realized something—I had spent years gaining valuable knowledge and experience in L.A., and I could use that to teach aspiring performers how to carve their own paths to success.

I also started revisiting a long-term goal that had always lingered in the back of my mind—creating and producing my own television show.

Once I was back home, my parents and I worked together to help me regain my sense of purpose and figure out my next steps. The directors of the Governor's School for the Arts, where I had attended high school, were impressed by my professional dance and performance credits. They offered me a faculty position to instruct high school students in the Musical Theatre, Dance, and Theatre departments.

I became a public high school teacher for Norfolk Public Schools, spending five years teaching at the same performing arts high school I had graduated from. Every day, my mission was to help passionate, talented performers refine their skills and create performances with top-tier technique. Just as important was guiding them in developing the kind of personal character that would connect with audiences and help them build meaningful, lasting careers in the entertainment industry.

Teaching professional-level performance skills came naturally, thanks to my training and experience with top industry professionals. At the start of each semester, my students were often uncoordinated, unfocused, and hesitant to push beyond their comfort zones. My job was to challenge them—to raise their standards in every single class.

The most challenging part of teaching wasn't just refining technique—it was helping students develop strong inner character. The entertainment industry is full of rejection and relentless pressure to meet others' expectations, which can take a toll on young, impressionable performers. I taught my students that success isn't about being the most beautiful or talented but about having a strong, kind, and passionate spirit. True success comes from combining education, training, respect for others, and gratitude for their talents—creating a foundation for both happiness and longevity in the industry.

Many of my students looked up to me as a mentor because of my experiences with celebrity performers and my appearances in films like *American Pie* and TV shows like *Fame*. I took that responsibility seriously, knowing that how I carried myself would set an example for them. I always emphasized that being in the entertainment industry should be about the love of the craft—not just the pursuit of fame and fortune.

My classes were highly structured from start to finish. Students quickly learned that being 15 minutes early was considered on time, arriving exactly on time was late, and walking in after class had started was completely unacceptable. Latecomers earned additional strengthening exercises—15 to 30 push-ups, depending on their tardiness. Side chatter during travel techniques or center floor activities had consequences too—push-ups or sit-ups. This level of discipline instilled focus, accountability, and a deep respect for the work.

Through teaching, I didn't just inspire others—I reignited my own passion for the performing arts and the journey of self-discovery. Watching my students grow became a reflection of my own evolution, reinforcing that the greatest achievements don't come from reaching a final destination but from fully embracing the process.

There were two golden rules that every student in my class was expected to follow.

Rule #1: Pay attention and stay focused—this was non-negotiable in a room full of performers constantly moving, spinning, kicking, and jumping. A moment of distraction could lead to injury. I also ingrained the importance of staying silent while receiving instructions and learning choreography. This ensured that students could fully absorb directions quickly without disrupting others who were also trying to learn.

Rule #2: Always have fun. Fun fuels passion, elevates performance levels, and makes every class an experience to look forward to. When performers enjoy what they're doing, it captivates audiences and brings their art to life.

My class was a **mental safe** space, designed to encourage students to believe in their potential and push toward their next highest goal. I taught them to perform as if they were always in front of the biggest, most important audience. This mindset was built on a simple but powerful principle: **Treat every class like an audition and every audition like a class.**

At an audition, you give **125%** to book the gig. In class, you give **125%** of your technique, discipline, and respect for others who share your craft. That level of commitment separates good performers from great ones.

At auditions, performers often showcase their highest levels of focus, presentation, technique, passion, audience connectivity, and performance skills. These elements should be practiced with the same intensity in every class. By consistently embracing this philosophy, students develop a foundation of professionalism that ensures nerves, anxiety, fear, or excitement never compromise their execution—whether in class, at an audition, during a taping, a broadcast, or a live performance.

Teaching my students this blend of positive mental focus, respect for others, self-pride, technique, and professionalism was always rewarding. By the end of each semester, they showed up on time, exuded exceptional talent, demonstrated refined technique and performance skills, and carried themselves like top-level professionals.

Nothing brought me more joy than assigning them well-earned grades on their quarterly report cards, knowing I had played a role in educating, shaping, and inspiring their careers in the performing arts.

Despite the numerous setbacks and disappointments of not reaching my own goals in the entertainment industry in Los Angeles, I chose not to embrace frustration, regret, or negativity. Instead, I took the opportunity provided by the Governor's School for the Arts to educate and inspire students. I embraced the chance to carry an aura of intention, greatness, and positivity.

By the end of my five-year tenure at the Governor's School for the Arts, I had become a beloved teacher and choreographer. I taught hundreds of students across performing arts, dance, theatre, and television. I also achieved my goal of producing an original television series and became recognized as an emerging television producer within the local community. The Governor's School for the Arts generously supported the first two seasons of my independently created television show, which laid the foundation for the success of broadcasting *American Dance Legend* on CBS and MyNetworkTV affiliates in the Hampton Roads area of Virginia.

The first television show I produced highlighted a tour to local schools and featured students from the Governor's School for the Arts. One of my students and co-stage performer, Grant Gustin, later became a global celebrity, starring in the television series *The Flash*. Grant appeared in the first television show I ever executive produced, *Fever*. He is an extraordinary, multi-talented performer with a heart of gold and a tenacious spirit. His success—winning a Teen Choice Award, being featured on *Glee*, and starring in *The Flash*—is a testament to his infectious personality and dedication to his craft. I remain humbled, proud, and supportive of my friend Grant and hope that I had even a tiny spark of impact on and inspiration for his performance talents. I am grateful to have been one of his performing arts teachers and to have shared stages and screens with him.

I experienced an internal shift from being a driven entertainer, eager to reach the top of the television, music video, and theatre worlds, to becoming an impactful, nurturing educator. I became self-aware of my true gifts and strengths, realizing that sharing my knowledge, education, and experiences with aspiring entertainment industry students was far more fulfilling than chasing a single golden opportunity for fame.

It is of utmost importance to remain connected with your innermost thoughts and physical actions, as they dictate the vibrations of energy you carry and project in life. Your energy impacts others, whether positively or negatively. Choose to be kind, genuine, forgiving, and nurturing to yourself. This approach sets the tone for how others within your path will treat themselves.

The way you carry yourself every day matters. The way you treat yourself every day matters. The way you treat others every day matters. Developing self-awareness in these three areas will guide you through life's challenges and obstacles, enabling you to achieve resolutions and victories as a high-level achiever. You will embody the armor of a heroic character and become an unstoppable warrior. Be self-aware.

"

"Choose to be
kind, genuine,
forgiving, and
nurturing to yourself."

Habit 9:

Be Self-Aware

Steps Toward Becoming Highly Self-Aware

Focus on Your "Internal Self-Awareness" This is how you view yourself.

Recognize your thoughts and answer these questions:

What are you thinking about (the present, the past, the future, absentmindedness, etc.)?

_____

_____

_____

_____

Why are you thinking your current thoughts (motivations, triggers, etc.)?

_____

_____

_____

_____

What physical actions and movements are you making (swaying, stiff, relaxed, jittery, etc.)?

_____

_____

_____

_____

_____

What is your body language (arms crossed timid, standing tall with posture confident, etc.)? _____

_____

_____

_____

What is your body temperature (hot, cold, sweaty, comfortable, etc.)? _____

_____

_____

_____

_____

How are you feeling (sad, happy, energized, confused, etc.)? _____

_____

_____

_____

_____

_____

_____

What is the presence of your feelings (familiar, new, repetitive, etc.)? _____

_____

_____

_____

_____

_____

_____

**Focus on Your "External Self-Awareness"
This is how others view you.**

**Identify others' perceptions of you
without bias and answer these questions
honestly:**
How is this person treating you (kindly,
harshly, connecting, distancing, etc.)?

_____

_____

_____

_____

What is the intent of this person's
connection with you (friendship, personal
gain, love, revenge, etc.)? _____

_____

_____

_____

Who is driving the conversations between you both (you, that person, a third party, etc.)? _____

_____

_____

_____

How is this person reacting to you (understanding, indifferent, passionate, etc.)? _____

_____

_____

_____

How does this person value you (with care, not at all, fraudulently, monetarily, etc.)?

_____

_____

_____

_____

What kind of triggers does this person evoke (joy, depression, abuse, fulfillment, etc.)?

_____

_____

_____

How is this person impacting you (mentoring, wasting time, sparking growth, etc.)?

_____

_____

_____

How is this person representing you to others (introducing, shaming, praising, bashing, etc.)? _____

_____

_____

_____

Balance Your Internal and External Self-Awareness:

By being consistent and persistent in toggling between your internal and external self-awareness, you will:

- Make better decisions.
- Become a profound leader.
- Act boldly and confidently.
- Vibrate on a higher frequency.
- Stand out above the crowd of unaware people.

Reflection

Chapter 10:

THE BUILDING BLOCKS TO BUILD YOUR EMPIRE

A s I progressed through high school, during my second year, I was assigned to an English class with a teacher named Mrs. Barbara Whiteside. When I saw her name on my class roster for the semester, I cringed internally.

Mrs. Whiteside was known throughout the school as one of the strictest, most direct, and unpleasant teachers you could have. She had a reputation for running a tightly controlled classroom—no unnecessary movements allowed, no speaking without permission, and absolutely no horseplay. Unfortunately, I was unable to change my schedule, so on the first day of class, I mentally prepared myself for a miserable experience.

Over the first few weeks, however, Mrs. Whiteside began to ask me detailed questions about the work I turned in. These questions often led to conversations where I sought her guidance and feedback on meeting her expectations, which always seemed higher for me than for most of my classmates.

Determined to surpass her expectations, I worked hard to deliver polished assignments, occasionally surprising her with creative, unconventional content. To my surprise, as the semester progressed, I found myself enjoying her class. While many of my classmates dreaded attending, I began to look forward to it. Our interactions developed into a unique student-teacher relationship.

Mrs. Whiteside went above and beyond to advise and guide me, not only in academics but also in leadership. For instance, juniors at our school weren't allowed to have a dance like the seniors. During a random conversation, she suggested I propose a junior class dance to the school board. I took her advice and led the charge to create and execute the school's first junior class dance.

To my surprise, Mrs. Whiteside became the primary supporter of the event, working alongside me. Though organizing the dance required a lot of effort and overcoming several obstacles, the final event was a huge success, enjoyed by both the junior class and their families. This experience taught me a valuable lesson: never let others' opinions about someone shape your perception of them before giving them a chance.

Mrs. Whiteside continued to stay connected with me, even during summer breaks. While vacationing out of state, she would occasionally send me postcards or letters to check in and see how I was enjoying my summer. Achieving the high standards she set for me in her challenging English class required focus, creativity, critical thinking, and determination. As an adult, I often receive compliments on my articulate speech and expressive writing, which I largely attribute to her mentorship.

Had I listened to my classmates and distanced myself from Mrs. Whiteside, I would have missed out on an incredible mentor. By taking the time to build a relationship with her, I profoundly improved my public speaking, writing, and leadership skills. These skills not only enriched my own school experience but also had a lasting impact on my life.

Another lifelong mentor I encountered was Chip Gallagher, the chairman of the Performing Arts Department at the Governor's School for the Arts in Virginia. Chip was a professional entertainer, composer, and the visionary behind the renowned musical theater department at the Governor's School for the Arts.

Chip exuded energy and positivity, with extraordinary talent as a pianist and singer. While his demeanor was generally calm and supportive, he had little patience for distractions or lack of focus. If you weren't doing what he asked, his piercing eye contact and stern expression made it clear he meant business.

Chip accepted me into his department during my freshman year of high school, just before I moved from Pennsylvania to Virginia with my parents. During our first summer rehearsals, I was in awe of the professional-level performances led by the upperclassmen. Their polished routines inspired me as we freshmen were spread throughout the background of most choreographed scenes.

After my first year, Chip created a new role for me: production manager. This position was a perfect match for my leadership skills and responsibilities within the traveling performance group, The Voices of Virginia. As production manager, I oversaw sets and equipment, managed travel and accommodations, and ensured all students were accounted for during rehearsals, performances, and tours.

Chip's mentorship extended beyond our department activities. He supported my personal ambitions and even composed an instrumental track for one of my first singles as a recording artist. Our collaboration was seamless, and I strove to meet his high expectations. Just when I thought I had reached them, he would challenge me further.

One day, Chip called me into his office for a conversation that took me by surprise. He began by asking if I had ever heard the phrase, "Don't get laid where you get paid." When I admitted I hadn't, he explained his concern: he had heard rumors about my growing list of intimate relationships with other students in the department.

While I was initially shocked by the conversation, I couldn't deny the truth of what he'd heard. At the time, I was a teenager managing leadership responsibilities, teenage hormones, and personal relationships. Chip explained that my behavior could undermine my leadership role and create unnecessary complications.

I took his advice to heart and made a conscious decision to avoid relationships within the department. I learned that as a leader, others' reactions—whether anger, envy, or jealousy—could add unnecessary challenges to an already demanding role. By focusing on my responsibilities and maintaining professionalism, I grew as a leader and avoided potential conflicts.

I'm sure it was very uncomfortable for Chip to step up to the plate and have that tough conversation with me, but it remains a value of mine some twenty years later as an adult in my active leadership roles.

Chip and I continually challenged each other in our working relationship to reach the best of our abilities. Chip challenged me with greater responsibilities, higher expectations, and new opportunities. I challenged Chip to consider deeper thought processes to positively impact the students in his department. I also pushed Chip outside of his comfort zone with independent projects that I produced, which were often outside his usual genres.

Chip and I have a long-standing, unique relationship where we can be friends in the outside world and still maintain a professional relationship at work. As a public high school teacher, Chip was my boss.

Chip remains a top inspiration in my life and career. He has guided and nurtured the pathway to success for many of his students in entertainment careers. Television celebrity Grant Gustin, Tony Award winner Adrienne Warren, and Broadway star Anthony Green are among the several students I have performed with or taught while at The Governor's School for the Arts. I am sure if you spoke with Grant, Adrienne, or Anthony, they would all profoundly express the same heartfelt gratitude for Chip's extraordinary mentorship, inspiration, and education.

One time, I was booked as the lead actor in a television commercial for a local Chevrolet car dealership. At the advertising agency that hired me, a very high-energy and spirited man named John Langlois was in charge. John, the owner of the advertising agency, was demanding but professional, leading his team with clear expectations and detailed direction for every move.

John had a magnetic personality that immediately connected with others. He was the kind of person you didn't want to upset, yet his kind and compassionate nature was so contagious that it captivated everyone he came across.

I worked with John closely during the script rehearsal for the commercial shoot. As the producer, John was very particular about how I should emphasize certain words. He also provided clear guidance on when to make eye contact with the camera and when to smile at specific moments in the script.

The executives from the car dealership and John's advertising agency team worked closely to create and film a successful television commercial. The ad aired frequently in the Hampton Roads cities of Virginia, where I was living at the time. I became known as "Karma the Car King" with the "deal of the day." I practiced that line and the rest of the script so often that I even dreamed about delivering it in front of a crowd of car-buying customers. One night, I woke up and realized it wasn't a dream—the commercial was actually playing on television.

John had a rare gift for creating powerful messages and connecting talent, businesses, and customers like no one else I've encountered. I was completely captivated by the ease with which he ran his agency and the expertise he brought to everything he did.

During a casual conversation, I shared my long-held dream of producing my own television show, a goal I had been pursuing since high school. Before I could even finish explaining, John assured me he could secure broadcast time for my show. About a year later, that's exactly what he did.

Fever was a 30-minute variety show that spotlighted incredible singers, dancers, and actors. With the help of several schools, businesses, and John's agency, my production company recorded the episode and aired it on a television station in Hampton Roads, Virginia. After this one-time show aired, John's mentorship and encouragement made me realize I had the ability to create, produce, and broadcast my own television series.

Moving forward, John and his agency teamed up with me and my production company to create and air two seasons of my television series, *American Dance Legend.* John secured broadcast time for the first season on a CBS affiliate and continued with another major network affiliate for the second season in Hampton Roads. While John was eager to help me achieve my broadcasting goals, I worked just as hard to bring exposure, client growth, and support to his agency.

I shifted from being hired talent to becoming a partner with John's agency for my television series. John and I built both a professional and personal relationship that played a key role in my life at that time. He not only gave me high-profile opportunities but also became a mentor and a trusted confidant for personal matters.

After my father passed away, John reached out, sensing I needed support. He spent an entire day just listening, offering his presence, and encouraging me to keep climbing the steps of my life. That day, he even took me to an upscale Brazilian steakhouse, where servers kept bringing food until I flipped a red-painted stand to signal them to stop. John's presence, our conversation, and the endless spread of high-quality food lifted my spirit and brought much-needed comfort to my heart.

By watching and learning from John's sharp business instincts and relentless drive, I built a strong partnership with him and his associates. Though the journey required serious effort and had its challenges, it became the bedrock of my growth in business leadership and ownership. John's partnership left me with an invaluable lesson: sometimes, you have to embrace discomfort to find your true comfort.

After broadcasting two seasons of *American Dance Legend,* I received an opportunity to expand the show through a production company in Orlando, Florida. Not long after moving there, I met Alan Ashe, a lively and expressive man with a contagious smile and laugh. From the start, we shared an unmistakable energy. During our first conversation, Alan learned I was new to the area and working on the third season of my show with a well-known production company he was already familiar with.

Alan, an entertainment executive at Disney for over 20 years, was the heart of the evening. He graciously introduced me to his friends and associates at the venue, unknowingly setting the stage for what would become a lasting partnership and friendship.

Alan often invited me to local events, from intimate live jazz sessions to massive gatherings at his estate—including his legendary Halloween parties. Dressing up for his parties and seeing Alan's hilarious costumes became an annual highlight.

Beyond the fun, Alan genuinely invested in my entertainment goals and growth as a motivational speaker. He even played a key role in helping Disney book me as a lead actor in a video shoot through my talent agency. In return, I worked to support Alan's projects, including getting the owner of my talent agency into his department's talent pool for future productions.

One of my favorite memories was hosting Alan's birthday party at a local restaurant. Even though he was hesitant at first, I made sure to transform the venue into a full-blown entertainment space for what turned out to be one of his most unforgettable birthday bashes.

The night had everything—live band, DJ, karaoke, and, of course, me as the host and Master of Ceremonies. Alan was surrounded by family, friends, and longtime associates, and for hours, he danced, sang, and laughed like I had never seen before.

True to form, Alan kept insisting on giving me money to cover the equipment and DJ I had arranged. I shut him down immediately, telling him to mind his business, enjoy his celebration, and let me take care of the rest.

Alan and I were, most times, like two peas in a pod. Although Alan is several years older than me, our age gap doesn't show in the fun-filled journeys we shared together. Alan and his production company played a key role in creating, developing, and launching my motivational speaking career. As the creative producer he is, he assisted in shooting, scripting, and producing my first motivational video, which was used to promote my speaking at events.

Alan is a fan of Texas Roadhouse and often visited the Kissimmee and Orlando locations where I worked. When he was celebrating his engagement with his fiancée, I coordinated a small surprise celebration for them, thoughtfully executed by my team of servers, hosts, and managers at the restaurant.

Alan witnessed and shared experiences with me during the highest points of my life and career as an entertainer, producer, and restaurant operator. Unfortunately, he also stood by me during the lowest points of my life and career. I was facing several major setbacks, which plunged me into a severe state of long-term depression. I had given up on trying to succeed, and Alan stayed connected with me, even though I had distanced myself from many of my closest friends and associates.

Alan was deeply concerned about my health and offered to take me to a hospital to address the severe depression consuming my mind and daily life. He even reached out to my mother, who was living out of state, and urged her to come to town to help me.

Because of Alan's unwavering support and genuine friendship, he and my mother encouraged me to check into a hospital to protect myself from the suicidal thoughts I was struggling with. During this period, I had mentally given up on myself and the world. I left my restaurant career, lost my home, had my car repossessed, and was living on benches and out of my storage unit during the lowest point of my downfall.

Once again, Alan went above and beyond to help me. He not only provided me with a place to sleep but also offered me a guest apartment on his property for a short while.

Facing Alan during this time was incredibly difficult. Seeing the transition from a successful and happy lifestyle to needing help with basic necessities was deeply embarrassing. It was demoralizing because it didn't reflect the strong, passionate, positive, and determined person he had known me to be for years.

While I stayed with Alan, he sat me down in his living room for one of the most intense conversations I'd ever had as an adult. He told me my poor choices had led to my downfall and urged me to adopt a broader perspective. Alan reminded me of the great potential I had as a business operator and entertainment producer. He inspired me to prioritize my mental health and work toward rebuilding my life and career.

At that moment, I saw for the first time in years the vision of greatness I wanted to continue striving for in life. I was reminded of my abilities and blessings.

After knowing Alan for approximately nine years, this was the most powerful and life-changing moment he had given me. It was his kindness, steady voice, vision, and unwavering support that pushed me to rise above life's challenges and inspire others through my journey. Today, I stand mentally and physically strong, living as my highest, truest, and best self. A casual introduction one evening turned into an incredible, life-saving friendship, and for that, I will always be deeply grateful. Thank you, Alan.

When I first moved to Orlando to produce the third season of my television series *American Dancing Legend* with a well-known production company, I still needed a basic income to cover my daily expenses. Although I had stepped away from my seven-year career path toward becoming a managing partner with Texas Roadhouse, they fully supported my decision to chase my dreams. They even gave me a recommendation and referral to work part-time as a local store marketer at their new location in Kissimmee, Florida—just outside Disney World.

When I arrived, I met the managing partner of the store, a man named Adam Conrad. Adam was Caucasian, a little over six feet tall, around 200 pounds, and appeared both mentally and physically strong. He had a focused, no-nonsense demeanor.

At first, Adam came across as slightly intimidating. His communication was straight-faced and razor-sharp, and his presence commanded attention. Still, he accepted me onto his team as a second local store marketer, given my years of experience in the same role at other stores in Virginia. By the time I joined, the store was already six weeks into its grand opening.

Adam was highly intelligent and multi-talented. He had previously held a Florida market kitchen operator title with the company and brought a level of knowledge and operational expertise I hadn't encountered during my earlier years with Texas Roadhouse. This high-profile location—just outside Disney World—was one of the busiest in the company, standing out among more than 500 locations nationwide.

At first, Adam's management style felt incredibly intimidating. He was like Chef Gordon Ramsay—pushing you to be your best, refusing to accept anything less than excellence, and demanding peak performance. While most of the nearly 200 opening team members experienced his aggressive, military-style leadership, I was spared much of that intensity.

The store's location catered heavily to tourists, a stark contrast to the more community-driven areas where Adam and I had previously worked. Stores near shopping plazas, schools, and residential neighborhoods typically thrived on standard marketing strategies and sales tactics. But those same approaches fell flat in this high-traffic vacation hub.

Adam challenged me to rethink everything I knew about marketing, building partnerships, and driving sales. He pushed me to start from scratch and develop a plan tailored to our one-of-a-kind location. As the local store marketer, I represented the Kissimmee store to businesses, organizations, and guests. The biggest challenge? Most guests were tourists who only visited for a few weeks a year, making it nearly impossible to build lasting relationships.

I pitched various programs to Adam to boost sales, and while he approved some, his usual response to many of my ideas was, "No, that's not the answer. Think bigger." After nearly a year of trial and error, the light bulb Adam had been pushing me to turn on finally clicked.

I realized that the most stable, year-round residents in the area were hotel clerks and vacation sales representatives—the very people I had already been building relationships with. Using this insight, I created a multi-layered program centered on strategic partnerships with hotels and travel representatives.

I requested an above-average marketing budget to bring this program to life. To my surprise, Adam approved it—but with conditions. He drilled into me the importance of timing supply orders, typically at the start of each month, and emphasized buying in bulk to cut costs over time.

Adam met with me weekly to go over my progress. At every stage of our store's growth, he pushed me to think beyond the obvious and instilled skills critical to running a multi-million-dollar business.

The program I created became a massive success. Over several years, it drove significant, sustained sales increases and delivered a strong return on investment.

Eventually, Adam offered me a full-time position on his management team. At first, I was hesitant—I was still focused on producing the third season of my series. But when he offered to double my pay for essentially the same work I was already doing, my decision became a no-brainer. I accepted without hesitation.

As a Service Manager, I enjoyed working at such a high-profile restaurant in the heart of Orlando's vacation scene. One day, while I was expediting entrées, Adam worked the broil grill, as he often did. He was one of the most skilled broilers I'd ever seen—capable of cooking over 100 steaks at once with incredible precision.

During the dinner rush, a server brought back a steak that needed to be re-cooked. Following standard procedure, I wrote the details on a ticket and sent it to Adam along with the plate. As expected, I also verbally explained what the guest said was wrong.

Minutes later, Adam turned to send the re-cooked steak back. But in a sharp tone, he made a cutting remark about the situation and aggressively tossed the plate through the window toward me. I caught it, but it slipped from my hands and shattered across the station, scattering sharp porcelain shards everywhere.

In that moment, I was stunned. Amazingly, I wasn't injured, but the scene left me furious. Struggling to keep my professionalism intact, I walked out of the restaurant during the peak dinner rush to cool off. What started as a short walk turned into an hour-long escape. My phone buzzed with calls from colleagues who had witnessed the incident and were worried about me. I reassured them—I just needed time to calm down.

When I finally returned toward the restaurant, I found myself standing at my car. I decided not to go back inside. Instead, I drove home, needing time to process my frustration.

A few days later, Adam called. He acknowledged that I was upset and apologized, claiming the plate had slipped. I didn't let that slide. I firmly told him that his aggressive behavior was not only disrespectful but also disrupted operations and could have caused serious injuries.

I made sure Adam understood my heart—I had worked tirelessly, day in and day out, for years, running his restaurant exactly as he envisioned, whether he was in the store or not. I told him that in my fifteen years of restaurant operations, I had faced countless situations, conflicts, and emergencies, but never—not once—had I been so disrespected as to have a superior, let alone a mentor, toss a plate at me.

Adam invited me to meet with him at the restaurant, and I agreed. During our conversation, I laid everything out—I explained, in detail, why I was so frustrated and why I had seriously considered leaving a team I had once been so proud to be a part of.

Adam listened and then opened up. He admitted that he had been dealing with personal issues that day, which had affected his behavior at work. He assured me it had nothing to do with me personally and offered a sincere apology. In turn, I apologized for letting my frustration get the best of me and for leaving the team short-handed during that shift and the following few days.

It was, without a doubt, one of the most awkward, difficult, and uncomfortable conversations I had ever had with a high-profile owner in the company.

From that experience, I learned that even the most high-level leaders are still human, with personal challenges and flaws that can sometimes impact their work performance. I also realized the importance of addressing conflicts with honest, calm communication while making the effort to understand the other person's perspective. Most importantly, I learned that in any professional relationship, it is not only acceptable—but sometimes necessary—to say, "I'm sorry."

Fortunately, Adam was not the type to micromanage. Unlike some owners, he trusted me to run the front of the house as I saw fit, stepping in only when he had specific expectations regarding financials and results.

In our weekly manager meetings, I would highlight the team's wins and opportunities, such as steadily increasing check averages and guest counts. But Adam never settled for the status quo. He would respond with direct challenges like, "Yes, but we still have the issue of large parties not being seated quickly enough, and the flip time between seating new guests after those large parties keeps crashing the kitchen. Fix it, Karma."

Operating in a high-traffic vacation area, our store took the concept of large parties to another level. Groups leaving the local theme parks often arrived in waves of 20 to 40 guests—or sometimes even more. The restaurant's prototype design was built for small parties of six or fewer, making this a daily logistical challenge. Yet Adam held me accountable for finding a solution.

Working closely with the front-of-house service team and leadership, I helped devise strategies to streamline large-party seating, ensuring smoother operations while maintaining guest satisfaction.

I was thrilled with the progress our team had made and eager to share our successes with Adam during our weekly manager meeting. Yet, deep down, I knew better than to expect him to be satisfied—his relentless drive for improvement meant there would always be another challenge.

As I presented our improved performance metrics and outlined our new strategies, I hoped we could shift focus to other goals. Instead, Adam nodded and said, "Well, that's great, but now I want you to become a master of the plan."

For the entire summer season—our busiest time of year—he assigned me to personally manage the front door, overseeing the seating of all parties, large or small, from opening at 4 p.m. to closing at 10 p.m.

I was shocked by Adam's decision—it pulled me away from key operational responsibilities like visiting guest tables, resolving issues, maintaining dining room efficiency, and coaching team members. Adam insisted I delegate those duties to my assistant managers and hourly supervisors for the summer.

Like anyone receiving an uncomfortable directive from their boss, I wasn't exactly thrilled to be made a "master host." By the end of that summer, the entire team and I were both physically and mentally drained.

However, our store repeatedly won **Store of the Quarter** in our Florida market and shattered company records for the highest sales volume and guest count in the country—week after week. Looking back, Adam's decision to station me at the host stand for an entire summer was one of the best things for my career. It forced me to master the intricate strategies, challenges, and flow of consistently seating large parties in a restaurant designed for much smaller groups.

Because of this success, our restaurant became the go-to choice for large parties in a highly competitive vacation market. Sales continued to soar, leading to corporate approval for a remodel that added an additional dining room.

Adam championed my goal of becoming a managing partner. He advocated for my promotion, placed me second-in-command, and gave me full access to the company's top leadership strategies. More often than not, he left the business in my hands, telling me, **"Karma, run it like you own it."**

Because of Adam's mentorship and advocacy, a 12-year goal became reality in August 2017: I was promoted to **Managing Partner/Owner** of America's top-rated steakhouse chain, **Texas Roadhouse** in Orlando, Florida. That moment forever changed my life and career, opening doors to rare opportunities for both me and my family.

Yes, I put in the years of hard work and dedication, but meeting a seemingly random character named **Adam Conrad**—someone who saw my potential, believed in me, and championed my growth—was just as pivotal. His guidance helped me build a solid foundation and ultimately achieve my dreams. **Thank you, Adam!**

66

"Be fearless in sharing
your innermost
self with those
who matter most."

The mentorship I received from **Mrs. Whiteside, Chip, John, Alan, and Adam** has been instrumental in shaping my character, leadership, and success. Their wisdom continues to guide me, proving that strong relationships have the power to leave a lasting and meaningful impact on the journey to building your empire.

Building relationships isn't always easy. It can be challenging, time-consuming, even intimidating—especially if you're introverted and find the process personally invasive. But I encourage you to approach relationship-building with an open heart and a mindset of **positive intent** because the rewards can be exponential.

Whether with family, friends, colleagues, partners, or neighbors, meaningful relationships take effort. **Don't shy away from that work.** When you intentionally cultivate connections, you develop a habit that leads to **abundance, peace, fulfillment, and joy.**

You were placed in this world to grow, evolve, and reach your **full potential**. And that journey isn't meant to be walked alone. True growth comes from supporting the people beside you and embracing those who cross your path—because some connections are not just meaningful but **meant to be.**

Sometimes, **true bravery** means looking back—reaching out to those who once connected with you deeply, even if you didn't fully recognize their purity and significance at the time. In those moments, you can only hope **it's not too late.**

But why wait until you're left wondering if a connection has slipped too far away? **Be courageous now**. Be fearless in sharing your innermost self with those who matter most. Be intentional in understanding the depths of the people you care about. **Approach each relationship with care, grace, acceptance, and an open heart.**

Strong, meaningful, and lasting relationships don't just happen—they are built. And no one will build them for you. Put yourself in the driver's seat. **Take action.** Initiate, nurture, and strengthen the connections that enrich your life.

BUILD RELATIONSHIPS—BECAUSE THEY ARE THE FOUNDATION OF EVERYTHING.

Thank You for Being a Part of This Journey!

If *Rebound, Succeed, and Win* has inspired or captivated you, I would be truly honored if you could share your thoughts with a review on Amazon, Goodreads, or any platform where this book is available. You can also leave a review directly on my website at **KarmaButler.XYZ.**

Your feedback not only helps others overcome their own challenges but also empowers them to turn their dreams into reality.

Thank you for your time, love, and support—I deeply appreciate it. I can't wait to connect with you again in the next book!

With Sincere Gratitude,

Karma Butler

Habit 10:
Build Relationships

Steps for Better Communication in Relationships to Strengthen and Grow Your Bonds

Listen with Purpose
Give your full attention, without interrupting or immediately inserting your own thoughts or emotions. _____

_____

_____

Read Between the Lines
Pay attention to body language and emotional cues to understand how the conversation is affecting the other person. _____

_____

_____

Be Honest and Transparent

Share your thoughts openly, truthfully, and with clarity.

_____

_____

_____

Communicate with Care

Express yourself with compassion, love, and genuine consideration for the other person's feelings. _____

_____

_____

Lead with Empathy

Step into their shoes, focusing on understanding rather than just responding.

_____

_____

_____

Respect Different Perspectives

Disagreements are natural, but dismissing or invalidating someone else's viewpoint is not.

Seek Resolution, Not Victory

Approach discussions with a mindset of compromise, aiming for a positive and constructive outcome.

Notes

_____

_____

_____

_____

_____

_____

_____

_____

_____

_____

_____

_____

_____

_____

_____

_____

_____

_____

_____

www.ingramcontent.com/pod-product-compliance
Lightning Source LLC
Chambersburg PA
CBHW070840120626
46556CB00002B/812